199

Facts About

Credit
Scores

By Jeff Zschunke

I DIDN'T LEARN THAT IN HIGH SCHOOL: 199 FACTS ABOUT CREDIT SCORES

1405 SW 6th Avenue • Ocala, Florida 34471 • Phone 800-814-1132 • Fax 352-622-1875
Website: www.atlantic-pub.com • Email: sales@atlantic-pub.com
SAN Number: 268-1250

Library of Congress Cataloging-in-Publication Data

Names: Zschunke, Jeff, author.
Title: I didn't learn that in high school : 199 facts about credit scores / by Jeff Zschunke.
Description: Ocala : Atlantic Publishing Group Inc., [2017] | Includes bibliographical references and index.
Identifiers: LCCN 2017005066 (print) | LCCN 2017021526 (ebook) | ISBN 9781620231746 (ebook) | ISBN 9781620231739 (alk. paper) | ISBN 1620231735 (alk. paper) | ISBN 9781620231746 (ebook) | ISBN 9781620232576 (library edition : alk. paper)
Subjects: LCSH: Credit ratings. | Credit scoring systems. | Consumer credit. | Consumer protection—Law and legislation.
Classification: LCC HG3751.5 (ebook) | LCC HG3751.5 .Z73 2017 (print) | DDC 336.3/4—dc23
LC record available at https://lccn.loc.gov/2017005066

Printed in the United States

PROJECT MANAGER AND EDITOR: Rebekah Sack • rsack@atlantic-pub.com
ASSISTANT EDITOR: Cathie Bucci
INTERIOR LAYOUT AND JACKET DESIGN: Nicole Sturk • nicolejonessturk@gmail.com

Reduce. Reuse.
RECYCLE.

A decade ago, Atlantic Publishing signed the Green Press Initiative. These guidelines promote environmentally friendly practices, such as using recycled stock and vegetable-based inks, avoiding waste, choosing energy-efficient resources, and promoting a no-pulping policy. We now use 100-percent recycled stock on all our books. The results: in one year, switching to post-consumer recycled stock saved 24 mature trees, 5,000 gallons of water, the equivalent of the total energy used for one home in a year, and the equivalent of the greenhouse gases from one car driven for a year.

Over the years, we have adopted a number of dogs from rescues and shelters. First there was Bear and after he passed, Ginger and Scout. Now, we have Kira, another rescue. They have brought immense joy and love not just into our lives, but into the lives of all who met them.

We want you to know a portion of the profits of this book will be donated in Bear, Ginger and Scout's memory to local animal shelters, parks, conservation organizations, and other individuals and nonprofit organizations in need of assistance.

– Douglas & Sherri Brown,
President & Vice-President of Atlantic Publishing

Table of Contents

Introduction

L et's face it. Scores matter. Your entire life up to this point has been a series of challenges where the outcome is determined by a number. Don't think so? Think again. Everything, from sporting events and video games to school elections and the SAT, is affected by numbers, percentages, and scores. As you move on from high school, towards college or the workforce, there is another number you will be forced to deal with — your credit score.

This score is like your shadow. It follows you wherever you go. Some scores are good. Some scores are bad. A bad score isn't the end of the world. The good news is you can change it. To fix it, you first need to know how it's calculated.

As you get older, your financial activity is monitored. When you swipe your credit card, a small record is made in your collective consumer secret file. Every pizza, every concert ticket, every new pair of shoes, all of it. So who is responsible for this monetary surveillance? While you are probably assuming it's the government's job, your files are actually under the watchful eyes of private companies.

These companies can sell and distribute your financial files to other companies without you even knowing. There is no way to stop it. The information contained in these records could be a mistake and you wouldn't even know it. Right or wrong, you are responsible for the information in your file. For example, imagine the receipt from John W. Smith's snowboard vacation to Utah winding up in the file of Jon W. Smyth, a surfer from California who hates the cold. Everyone makes mistakes, even these big companies. However, when these companies make mistakes, it affects you. It can keep you from buying a car, renting an apartment, or being able to take out a loan for college.

So, who looks after your files? Who decides whether your score is good or bad? The answer is credit reporting agencies. There are three major players in the game of credit history: Equifax, Experian, and TransUnion. Think of them as coaches or team managers. They analyze and compile all of the information in your file and give you a credit score. Like a number on the back of a jersey, your credit score follows you around the field of life for all to see.

The information these companies track is not limited to just credit card information. They can track if you rent an apartment, apply for a job, or get car insurance. If you break your leg at a 24-hour dance marathon, that hospital bill gets neatly tucked into your report. Even topics not related to finance can affect your score. Suppose your sister borrows your library card to check out the latest bestseller, but loses the book and forgets to tell you. After a few months, the overdue fees start to stack up. While this incident isn't financial, it demonstrates how public records are part of your report as well.

These companies don't need to explain to you or anyone else how they pick your credit score. It's private. Like a secret family recipe, they can keep their ingredients for deciding the magic number out of view from the public.

With all of these hidden files being exchanged behind your back like you're in a spy movie, you may be wondering how you can possibly fight back. How can you be sure that the number you carry is the one you want? The answer is the Fair Credit and Reporting Act (FCRA). Think of it like a superhero created by the government to fight for your consumer rights. The Fair Credit and Reporting Act makes it possible for everyday people like you and me to finally peel back the curtain on these files and see what's inside. You can find mistakes and start to take the steps to change them. The FCRA helps ensure that your credit score isn't permanent.

This book will teach you all about the files these private companies hold containing your personal financial history. It will teach you how to improve your credit score by accessing your files and ridding them of any inaccurate information. Cleaning up your credit profile is the first step in improving your personal credit score. This book will also teach you what credit is, the different types of credit, and how it affects your score. It will discuss how major life events like college, a new job, or your first apartment impact your credit rating.

In the next nine chapters, we will dive deep into the wild world of credit scores. So, pull on your goggles and snorkel and hold your breath. Your exploration of the credit score ocean is about to begin!

CHAPTER 1

What Is a Credit Score?

A credit score is a number. While this definition is simple, calculating a credit score number is a very complicated business. Each credit score is generated by complex mathematical formulas called algorithms. When you decide to apply for a credit card or open a savings account at the local bank, a number will be generated for you too.

Fact #1: To be eligible to receive a credit score, you must have an account open for at least six months.

It all starts with your application. You supply personal information about where you live, your age, and any previous financial history you may have. This information is combined with other credit reports that may already exist about you. Once these reports are combined, they are processed in a computer using an algorithm to compare your application with the applications and reports of millions of other consumers just like you. The algorithm analyzes specific aspects of your history. It looks at your number of accounts, the types of accounts, late payments and debts, and after it is finished screening and processing all of this information, you are given points. In the end, the combined number of points assigned to your profile becomes your credit score.

> A credit score is a way for businesses to evaluate how responsible you are with paying back money that you borrow. These businesses can be organizations such as banks, credit unions, car dealerships, and sometimes retail stores. A good credit score is also used as a qualifier for certain jobs that require you have access to personal financial information or experience handling large amounts of cash. It can be very helpful to have a good credit score.
>
> —Amber Berry, certified financial education instructor and certified money coach

Not everyone has a credit score right away. It takes time for your history to process and be established among various credit reports. If your account history is shorter than six months, there isn't enough data to put into the algorithm, so you will not be able to get a credit score. But once you are eligible, this score becomes a way for financial institutions and other companies to gauge trust. The higher your score, the less risk involved.

Fact #2: The FICO score range is between 300 and 850 points.

The algorithms that determine your credit score are supplied by a California-based company known as Fair Isaacs Corporation, better known as FICO. The FICO scoring model is used by credit reporting agencies to compile your data and generate a three digit score. This score is reported to banks and credit card companies investigating your credit history. Depending on the company, you may pay to receive your score directly from them as well.

Most people with a positive credit history score in the upper end between 600 and 800 points. Barring any financial setbacks, your credit score will probably settle somewhere near the national average. Where you live plays an important role in your score as well. Cities in the Northern half of the United States display higher average scores than Southern cities.

Fact #3: The national average FICO score is 695.

Banks and credit card companies don't just pull names out of a hat to decide who they do business with. They let the FICO score make that decision for them. If you have a higher FICO score, you may be offered a bank account with a better interest rate or a credit card with a higher spending limit. If your score is on the lower end, you may be denied services. The bank or card company will use your credit score as the main reason.

As you can see, your FICO score is a major player in determining your ability to gain access to financial services. When a company looks at your score they are making a big decision. They are deciding how risky a bet you are. Since your score is determined by analyzing your past, what if your file contains a mistake? Before you go all-in and apply for a credit card or open an account, you'll want to investigate your own file. To do that, you'll need some help.

The Fair Credit Reporting Act (FCRA)

Your consumer credit file is made up of different records. Some of these records are public and can be found by making a formal request or searching public records. Some of these records are private and not freely available. Consumer reports are a mix of both private and public records.

When credit agencies started to gain access to consumer files containing both public and private records, the government made the decision to get involved. In 1970, the U.S government took action and wrote a law protecting consumer's credit rights. This law protects consumers by limiting the credit agencies access to private records and regulating how they use the reports in generating a credit score.

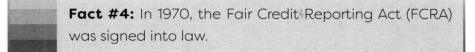

Fact #4: In 1970, the Fair Credit Reporting Act (FCRA) was signed into law.

The Fair Credit Reporting Act acts as law enforcement for the credit report agencies. It keeps the companies that distribute your credit report accountable. If you feel there may be an error somewhere in your credit file, the FCRA makes it possible for you to view its contents and take the steps necessary to repair it.

Over the years, the Fair Credit Reporting Act has been improved. There have been many updates to the law that help protect consumers even more. For example, you are now entitled to a free copy of your credit file once a year. This assists consumers by helping them inspect their credit information without having to pay. The new amendments also make it easier to alert the credit agencies if you feel you are the victim of fraud or identity theft.

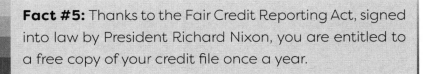

Fact #5: Thanks to the Fair Credit Reporting Act, signed into law by President Richard Nixon, you are entitled to a free copy of your credit file once a year.

Just as the law makes it easier for you to notify the companies of potential problems, it also requires the companies to notify you. Like a watchdog, credit agencies have enacted security notifications in their computer systems that attempt to sniff out any suspicious activity.

Perhaps the best improvement of all has come in response to credit card receipts themselves. Before the Fair Credit Reporting Act was passed, receipts from transactions displayed your full account number and expiration date. Imagine losing that receipt. Your full account number, clearly visible for anyone to steal! Today, all receipts only display the last 4 or 5 digits of your account number and your expiration date is no longer printed. This added measure of security has helped prevent countless acts of theft and fraud.

> **Fact #6:** The reason receipts from credit card transactions no longer display your full account number or expiration date is thanks to an amendment of the FCRA in 2003 called the Fair and Accurate Credit Transactions Act.

How Do I Check My File?

In the previous section, you learned that the Fair Credit Reporting Act provides one free copy of your credit file a year. So, how can you get a copy? Unlike the contents of these detailed files, the process is quite simple.

Fortunately, the government established a central distribution center for all free credit files. You can obtain your copy by phone, mail, or visiting their website, www.annualcreditreport.com. This centralized location makes the process much easier and you don't have to search for your file like a needle in a haystack.

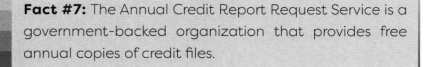

> **Fact #7:** The Annual Credit Report Request Service is a government-backed organization that provides free annual copies of credit files.

Once you receive your files, you may get offers from a credit agency sent along with it. These offers will be willing to sell you a credit score. Keep in mind that not all scores are created equal. Each company uses their own FICO scoring system to screen your credit file and give you a score. Your score may differ across all three bureaus, though it shouldn't be by a wide margin. The difference may come from the way each bureau captures information about you, or from the way information is weighted in their scoring system. If your scores vary wildly, that could be a red flag, and you should try to find out why.

> **Fact #8:** There are two types of credit reports: standard and investigative.

The differences between standard and investigative credit reports are rooted in their level of complexity. In your life you will most likely only encounter standard reports. These reports are a basic look at your personal financial history. They are a mix of personal financial history and public records. Investigative reports are much more detailed. They take a closer look at a person's history and their relationships. If you ever apply to work as an FBI agent, you can certainly look forward to receiving an investigative report.

A credit file and a credit report are not the same. Think of a book report. All of your notes and neon-pink-highlighted passages are like your credit file. The typed, double-spaced manuscript you turn in to your teacher is like the credit report.

A credit report is what the credit agencies sell to banks and credit card companies after they sift through the contents of your credit files. Much like your report for your teacher, not everything makes it into the final report.

Fact #9: The three biggest credit-reporting agencies in the United States are Equifax, Experian, and TransUnion.

Having access to an annual copy of your credit file for no cost is a huge advantage for a consumer. But, what if you need a copy more than once? The good news is you can still purchase an additional copy of your credit files from any of the three major players in the business. Equifax, Experian, and TransUnion are like the Mount Rushmore of credit reporting. These industry titans can help you with an extra copy of your file if you ever are in need. Remember: your file contains all of the documents and records the credit bureaus use to compile a report.

Fact #10: Even if you've already received a copy of your free annual credit file, you may still purchase a copy through any of the major credit reporting agencies.

These major leaders in the industry make money because banks and other companies are willing to pay for reports detailing your private history. When a bank or credit card company is helping someone they don't know anything about, they will pay top dollar for a glimpse into their past.

How Do I Get My Score and Report?

The credit reporting industry trifecta is composed of the credit file, the credit report, and the credit score. After a little research, getting access to your credit file is easy. Gaining access to a credit report is a little more complex and can come with a price tag. Credit reporting agencies will provide credit scores to consumers only after collecting a fee.

There are four main types of reported information that determine your credit score. The first type is how you have paid your credit obligations in the past. The second type is how much you owe on current credit obligations and how much credit you still have available. The third type is the length of time you have had accounts with creditors. The fourth type is the types of credit you have used. Applying for credit multiple times in a short amount of time can lower the score. There are up to 15 other factors that may be considered in computing credit scores. Some of these factors include your annual income, employment history, whether or not you have bank accounts, public record and collection items, credit inquiries, and more.

—JeFreda Brown, MBA, business consultant and CEO of Goshen Business Group, LLC

Fact #11: Unlike credit files, federal law does not require agencies to provide credit scores for free.

In the last section, you learned a little bit about credit scores and how they are calculated. You know that not all credit scores are created equal. This fact will become more evident once we examine the parts that make up your credit score.

Fact #12: Credit reporting agencies provide up to four reasons for their credit scores

When you receive your score, the credit reporting agency will also share with you up to four reasons why your score is what it is. These are called reason statements. Reason statements are worded descriptions for reason codes that are provided to whatever bank or company is reviewing your application.

Fact #13: There are more than 60 different reason codes available to credit reporting agencies to help explain the reasoning for a consumer's credit score.

If you are wondering why this seems familiar, think of your report cards. In school, your report cards contain letter or number grades. There is also a section for comments from your teachers. Just like your report card, the credit agency adds their own comments to your credit score transcript.

The reasons that often pop up on most credit scores deal with debts owed. For example, a consumer who was late paying their cell phone bill might get a reason code of 02 - Level of delinquency on accounts. Or maybe you have 15 different credit cards that you've been using to pay for all of your spring break trips; you might get a reason code of 05 - Too many accounts with balances. Don't worry, not all reason codes are negative. If you receive a high credit score, your reason codes will show positive remarks.

> **Fact #14:** Fair Isaac Corporation is responsible for developing the most widely used reason codes and statements.

If your credit score isn't quite what you had hoped and your reason codes aren't up to par, the agencies will provide some added guidance. Credit scores not only provide reason codes but help consumers by offering tips. These tips help consumers identify the problems with their score and put them on track to correct them.

> **Fact #15:** Reason statements can be both positive and negative.

It's important to establish credit early and use it responsibly. This doesn't mean open up 10 credit cards and max them all out. It means open up one credit card at a time, with a maximum of three over the course of one to three years. Use only half of what you are allowed to spend (maximum credit) and pay it off every month. A good general rule is don't buy it if you don't have the money in the bank to pay the bill at the end of the month.

—Elysia Stobbe, mortgage expert and bestselling author

Online Access

Thanks to advances in technology, you are no longer limited to just paper copies of your credit files, reports, and scores. You can have digital access, all the time, from anywhere in the world.

There are two ways to go about this: you can go directly to the credit agencies and purchase information, or you can get it for free from several reputable companies. You're probably wondering why you would pay for something you could get at no charge. First, let's talk about what's available for free.

Most of us have learned to be suspicious of offers that promise something for "free." In many cases, we're right to be suspicious. Of course there are companies that will offer you "free" access to your credit report, but when you sign up, you have to put in your credit card number. Put down your wallet, and back away from the computer slowly.

There are also companies out there that believe the information on your credit report belongs to you, so you should have the right to access and monitor it. Three reputable sources for credit scores and reports are: Credit Karma, Credit.com, and WalletHub.

Credit Karma

Credit Karma gives you 24/7 access to your credit report for free, with scores from both TransUnion and Equifax. You can opt into activity notifications, and reports are updated weekly. Credit Karma gives you tips on improving your score and has a "score simulator" so you can see how your score may change based on activity in your report.

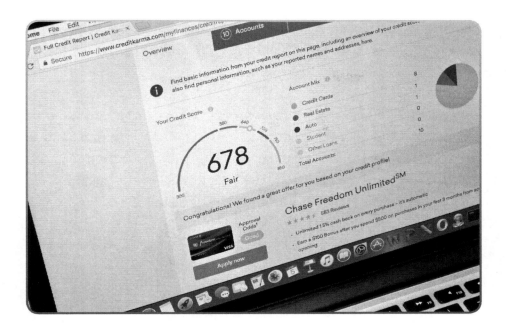

You do have to give some personal information so your identity can be verified, but you don't have to give your credit card number. Credit Karma receives a commission every time they successfully match up banks and credit card companies with their subscribers, so you pay nothing.

Credit.com

Credit.com also gives you two scores, one using the VantageScore 3.0 model, and one directly from Experian. Your score is updated monthly, you receive direct feedback about your score, and they provide tips to improve your standing. Once again, no credit card required!

WalletHub

WalletHub provides one score and report from TransUnion. There are many things that can influence your credit score, and WalletHub offers you a report-card-style letter grade on each of them, and an explanation of the grade if you need it. They do not charge for this service, as they make money the same way that Credit Karma does.

If you really want to be vigilant about your credit, sign up for Credit Karma and Credit.com accounts. You'll have access to information from all three credit bureaus, and if you combine that with your report from Annual-CreditReport.com, you can know what's happening in your credit file and catch signs of identity theft before it gets out of hand.

So those are the ways that you can keep a close eye on your scores and reports without any expense. Now, let's talk about the reasons you might need to pay a credit agency.

Credit Agencies

What if you've already experienced the trauma of identity theft? Maybe you're trying to rebuild your credit after some bad financial decisions. If you have reason to believe that your credit is in jeopardy, paying a credit bureau for copies of your file, or for other programs they offer, might be in your best interest.

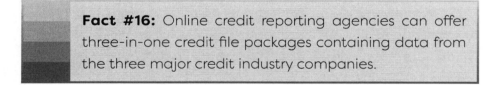

Fact #16: Online credit reporting agencies can offer three-in-one credit file packages containing data from the three major credit industry companies.

Perhaps you don't need an agency to tell you your score or give you a report, but the agencies have adapted to this new digital world by offering other services. All three bureaus, and the Fair Isaacs Corporation itself, offer forms of credit and identity monitoring. While these services carry a price tag, they are an excellent first line of defense in the war against identity theft. Also, if you're in the midst of credit recovery or identity theft, you may have to dispute information that's in your file or place a freeze on your credit report. Dealing with the agency directly may not be simple or fun, but since your credit can have a big impact on your future, it's worth the hassle.

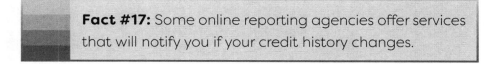

Fact #17: Some online reporting agencies offer services that will notify you if your credit history changes.

These new trends in the tech economy are proving to be vital to consumer credit success.

But Wait . . . There's More!

So far you've learned about credit reporting agencies and their roles in supplying information to businesses and consumers. However, banks and credit card companies are not the only industries who need to worry about risk. There are many specialty consumer-reporting agencies that supply companies with reports about consumers with a specific history. There are specialty consumer reporting agencies in many industries, but we are going to focus on a select few.

Check your checkbook

Next time you are standing in a checkout line, take notice of how people pay for their purchases. You will probably see mostly cash and credit transactions. What about checks? Have they become embarrassing like last season's fashion trend?

Sadly some people use writing checks to pay for goods as a quick and easy method of fraud. Think about it. I'll give you this piece of paper with an amount and my signature and you give me what I want. How does the seller know you have the funds to back it up?

> **Fact #18:** National check registries are specialty reporting agencies that deal with checking issues.

There are some specialty reporting agencies that deal specifically with problems related to writing and cashing checks. These registries operate as clearinghouses for information related to negative checking account behavior. They compile their information into a database which is accessible to other businesses who act as subscribers.

Many business owners find it is a huge advantage to belong to one of these registries as a subscriber. For example, imagine you are the owner of a grocery store and a customer wants to pay for their order by check. If you subscribe to one of the check registries you would be able to see if this individual has a negative reputation with regard to writing checks.

The house always wins

No one walks into a casino with a million dollars in their pocket. Even the wealthiest gamblers take advantage of a casino's credit programs. With such high stakes, casinos can't afford to just give away money to anyone to gamble with. A special reporting agency called Central Credit Services is the largest consumer database in the gaming industry. The information contained in their database is used to profile gamblers in their system and evaluate their level of risk.

Gamblers get many advantages from borrowing money from the casino. Interest-free lines of credit and numerous perks like free lodging and unlimited lunch buffets are just some of the bonuses shared by card sharks and dice rollers in the biggest U.S. casinos.

Guests who borrow the most money get the best rewards. Casinos are constantly competing with each other to reel in the bigger customers. The more money a gambler borrows, the more potential profits the casino will gain.

Fact # 19: To help track high-stakes borrowing, casinos give preferred guests "markers." A marker is a casino's line of credit account that monitors their gambling habits and houses their personal and private information.

Central Credit Services tracks reports generated by the use of markers on the casino floor. If a player is late in paying off a debt, has too many markers at numerous casinos, or demonstrates questionable behavior, a note is made in the CCS database. Over time, casinos are able to determine who the players with the best reputations are and can use this data to help increase their profits.

The doctor will see you now

Every time a new patient is treated in a hospital or a doctor's office, one of the first questions asked is, "Do you have insurance?" Medical bills can reach astronomical levels, and can strain a person's ability to pay on time, if at all. There's a specialty agency whose only job is to monitor your medical insurance history.

The Medical Information Bureau is a specialty reporting agency that collects and distributes files based on your medical insurance history. Hospitals can reference the MIB database whenever you check in at the front desk.

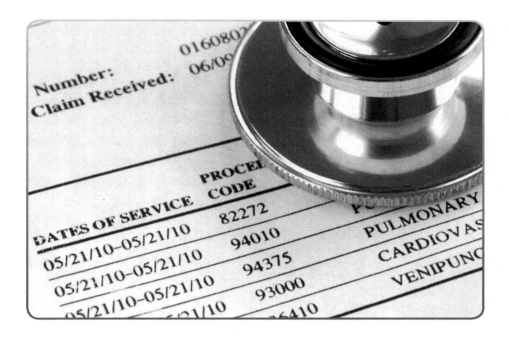

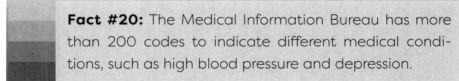

Fact #20: The Medical Information Bureau has more than 200 codes to indicate different medical conditions, such as high blood pressure and depression.

If you have a lengthy medical history, there is probably an MIB file in existence with your name on it. If you break your leg skateboarding, or check in with your doctor over asthma issues, a digital paper trail is started. The Medical Information Bureau has a variety of reason codes to indicate different medical conditions.

For rent

Landlords have a very difficult job. In the future, you may decide to rent an apartment with friends. Your landlord will talk with you and have some basic questions, but how can he or she trust you? How does he or she know you will pay on time each month?

Fact #21: A landlord can ask a tenant screening company to provide a report on individuals applying to rent a property.

Thanks to tenant screening companies, landlords can access a database containing a tenant's rental and payment history. After examining a report, if there are too many red flags, such as failure to pay on time or destruction of property, a landlord can choose not to rent their property to that individual.

> Past credit is a good predictor of future behavior. If you have a history of not paying your bills, you might not pay some of them in the future (unless you have a big life change). The same goes for good credit. If you have a history of paying your bills on time, you are likely to do the same in the future. If you have limited or no credit history, that is also taken into consideration.
> —Elysia Stobbe, mortgage expert and bestselling author

Now hiring

Some employers may ask to complete a background check on you before offering you a job. If an employer elects to run a check, you must be notified. When you are filling out an application, your boss may have you sign a form stating that a check into your work history will be performed.

Fact #22: It is unlawful for an employer to run a background screening on employees without their permission.

Employee screening services are not like the other specialty reporting agencies. They do not keep files on individuals. Because there is no database, you cannot request a copy of your employment history file. Employee screening services are more like private investigators. If asked by a business, they will go digging through your work history and prepare a report should any concerns arise.

CHAPTER 2

The Credit Report

There have probably been many times in your life when you needed to ask someone for something. Maybe it was something simple, like asking for extra toppings on an ice cream cone, or something more important like asking your parents to borrow the car for Friday night.

In the world of credit files, you don't need to ask. When you apply for that first credit card or take out that student loan you need for college, a credit file will be automatically generated for you. It can be a complicated process; your parents will probably want to help. Let them! They know what they're doing; they've been through it themselves many times before. Just remember that your credit file is YOUR credit file. Even if your parents pay your bills for you, the file is yours and yours alone.

Credit reporting agencies play a vital part in helping consumers make financial decisions. They keep you outfitted with different combinations of files, reports, and scores that help you throughout your financial life. While these institutions are vital to your credit score upkeep, they are still businesses. They are constantly in competition with each other and will offer competitive pricing and varying package combinations to attract you to their side. These agencies are in full battle mode over your consumer attention and you have to choose whose team to play on.

Fact #23: The credit reporting industry processes over four billion pieces of data per month.

The credit report is like a crystal ball. Companies use this report to look into your financial future. Your credit report paints a picture about your past and gives companies a sense of how to approach your relationship with them.

The information contained in your credit file is very important. If any information is inaccurate, you could have a very difficult time getting any financial assistance at all. With billions of pieces of data a month being processed by credit reporting agencies, it is crucial that the information in your files is correct.

What Is Credit?

Credit is an agreement over money. Banks and credit card companies give credit based on information contained in your credit report. Sometimes these companies will offer you credit without you even applying. If you have no credit history to examine, these companies will offer you a fixed amount of money known as your credit limit. These offers will usually be seen in your mailbox first, or maybe you've seen them at a sporting event or concert. You remember the cute guy or girl who asked you to sign up, and said you'd get a free t-shirt or beach towel?

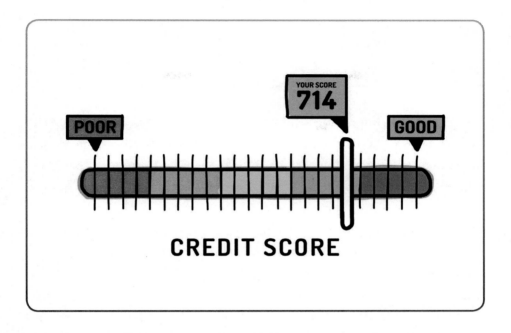

Fact #24: Credit is the ability to borrow money, based on the trust that it will be paid back.

It is important to remember that credit is debt. Yes, the dreaded "D" word! It is important to remember that all debt is not necessarily bad. Sometimes debt can help you attain or experience things you would never get to have any other way.

As a rule of thumb, it is recommended that the amount of credit used should not exceed 30 percent of the available credit limit. For example, if you have a credit limit of $1,000, you should try to keep the balance below $300.
—JeFreda Brown, MBA, business consultant and CEO of Goshen Business Group, LLC

Fact #25: There are two types of debt known as secured and unsecured.

Secured debt is linked to possessions or other tangible items. Examples include things like mortgages and car loans. If you borrow money for a house or a car and you don't pay back the money you borrow, the bank will take it away from you.

Unsecured debt is a bit trickier. The best example of unsecured debt is a credit card. If you use a credit card to make purchases but fail to pay the bill when it arrives each month, there is nothing for the company to take away. That doesn't mean that nothing happens. In the case of unsecured debt your credit files and reports would show these failed payments and your credit score would plummet. Remember, in the world of credit scores, reputation is everything.

The credit landscape can often seem intimidating or even scary. You may be tempted to avoid credit cards and loans altogether. Having no credit history is almost as bad as having a history of bad credit. You wouldn't lend five dollars to someone on the street and expect them to pay you back. If a company doesn't know you, how can they trust you?

Parts of a Credit Report

Fact #26: There are six main sections of a credit report. These include personal information, an account summary, public records, current finances, credit inquires, and an optional message.

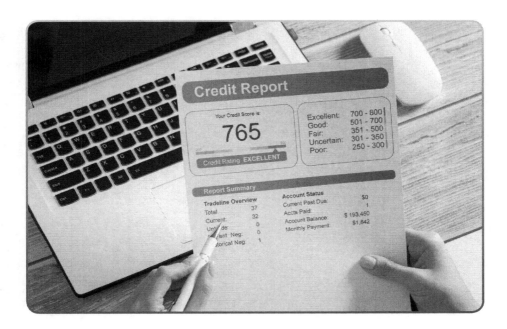

Credit reports are created by credit reporting agencies from the information contained in a consumer's credit file. Each agency uses their own design and format, but most reports contain the same areas of information. Though their individual titles may differ, credit reports contain the following sections:

Personal information

The personal information you supply is needed for identification purposes only. Each time you fill out an application, the personal information you enter is added to your credit file.

> **Fact #27:** Your personal information is not used as a means for evaluating your credit history.

This section contains six parts. They are:

1. Name

2. Social Security number

3. Date of Birth

4. Addresses

5. Employment History

6. Driver's License Information

> Your credit report has a great deal of personal information about you and your financial history. It will list all of the addresses you've lived, your Social Security number, and all of the open accounts that you currently have. Open accounts include credit cards that you have and loans you are paying back. If you have struggled in the past with keeping up with your payments, the credit report will also show anything sent to collections. Since these reports have such important information, it is a really good idea to check them often to ensure that there are no mistakes.
>
> —Amber Berry, certified financial education instructor and certified money coach

When filling out your personal information on credit applications, it is important to be as detailed as possible. For example, if you and one of your parents have the same name, make sure to add a suffix or middle name to your application.

Fact #28: Confusion over names is one of the biggest causes of credit file errors

Your address helps companies track your place of residence. Constantly moving from one place to another can be a red flag for a bank or credit card company and lead to them denying you credit.

Account summary

This section of the credit report is a summary of your financial background. It contains information about any open accounts, closed accounts, account balances, credit limits, and past payments. It is a condensed version of the account information contained in your credit files. The credit files information can be many pages long.

Public records

Credit reporting agencies will regularly check public records for information to include in your credit files. The records they choose to include will usually have a negative effect on your report. Public record information includes bankruptcies, mortgage issues, failure to pay taxes, and repossessions by collection agencies. Hopefully, you'll never have to deal with any of these public record issues, but in case you do, we will discuss them below.

Taxes

Uncle Sam will always get his share. It seems many people forget this and fail to pay taxes, resulting in what is called a tax lien. A tax lien occurs when a consumer can't pay their taxes and the government attaches the bill to their personal property. It's like having an extra mortgage on your house.

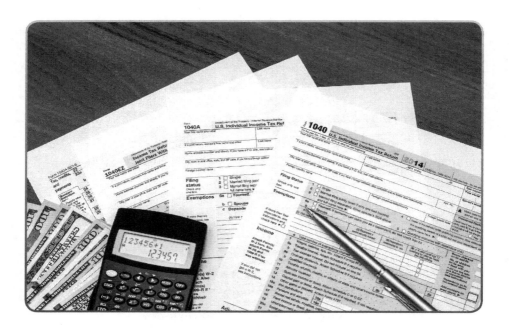

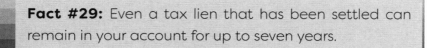

Fact #29: Even a tax lien that has been settled can remain in your account for up to seven years.

A tax lien in your credit file can do serious damage to your financial reputation.

Court decisions

If you ever find yourself on the wrong end of a lawsuit, a judge's decision against you can have a negative influence on your credit report. When a judge makes a decision in a case, he issues a judgment. The presiding judge awards a certain amount of money to be paid from one person to another. Judgments can remain in your credit file for up to seven years from the day in which the court enters them.

Fact #30: A judgment is a court decision about a lawsuit. If you have been involved in any litigation, it is a matter of public record and it could affect your credit score.

Bankruptcies

Declaring bankruptcy should only be considered as a last resort in dealing with financial hardships. While declaring bankruptcy effectively closes an outstanding account in the same way paying off a debt does, it will cause your credit score to go into freefall mode. Filing for bankruptcy can remain in your credit file for up to ten years.

Foreclosures

If you are unable to make the monthly payment on your home, your mortgage enters what is called foreclosure. Foreclosure is the process of taking possession of a property if a person is unable to keep up with their mortgage payments.

You and your lender don't want to arrive at this mortgage process crossroad. But, if you are consistently missing payments, they will have no choice but to report you to a credit agency and begin foreclosure proceedings.

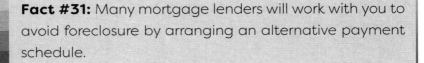

Fact #31: Many mortgage lenders will work with you to avoid foreclosure by arranging an alternative payment schedule.

Vehicle repossessions

Failure to make payments can cause you to lose more than just a good credit score. If you keep missing car payments, you could lose your ride. Just because a car is in your possession, doesn't mean it belongs to you.

The lender holds onto the paperwork until the loan for the car is paid off. At that time, the paperwork is transferred to the owner. No paperwork, no proof. Many state laws allow for lenders to repossess a vehicle without warning. You could wake up one morning and find yourself taking the bus.

Wage attachments

In some cases, the government can force you to pay back a debt without you even writing a check. If you do not set up a payment schedule with regard to any legal cases, the court can place a wage attachment on your employer's payroll.

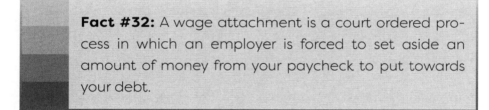

Fact #32: A wage attachment is a court ordered process in which an employer is forced to set aside an amount of money from your paycheck to put towards your debt.

A wage attachment is like a financial leech, sucking away your pay a little at a time. You'll find your pay to be a little lighter each week thanks to this tactic.

Student loans

Getting into college can be one of the most exciting experiences, but figuring out how to pay for it can be one of the most stressful. While most students start paying off their loans after college ends and they enter the workforce, not every student is that fortunate. Delinquent student loans may remain in your credit file for up to seven years. That is a long time after graduation to be dealing with a blemished report, especially during such a busy time in your adult life.

Arrests

While you wouldn't think of a criminal record as having an impact on your financial life, it can still find its way into your credit file. Most credit companies don't include information on arrests or convictions, but insurance companies and employers certainly have an interest in your past run-ins with the law.

Current and past history

Both current and past financial information is reported by banks and credit card companies. This section of your credit report includes detailed information on both open and closed accounts. Unpaid accounts may remain in your report for up to seven years. Paid or closed accounts may remain for up to ten years.

Your report will show the dates the accounts were opened, the types of accounts, account balances, and payment history.

Relationships can also play a role in your credit report. If you open any joint accounts in the future because you get married and you decide it is a wise financial move, the activity on those accounts will affect the credit reports of both you and your partner.

Fact #33: Debt accumulated between married couples becomes the responsibility of both spouses.

Medical insurance claims both past and present have a place in your credit report as well. If your insurance company fails to pay a claim to a hospital or doctor's office, you may find yourself in some financial hot water. If you aren't familiar with the out-of-pocket costs for medical procedures, a quick Internet search will surely shock you.

Fact #34: Disputes between consumers and medical insurance companies are not the responsibility of the service provider. They may attempt to collect from the individual if a medical insurance company fails to pay the bill.

Credit inquiries

Your credit report also contains a section dedicated to the number of times your information has been accessed. Each time an individual or banking institution examines your profile, a credit inquiry occurs.

Fact #35: A credit inquiry is a formal request to look at your credit file.

Alarms will go off in the minds of credit representatives if they see too many business inquiries listed in a row on your report. This may raise suspicion among those looking to approve your loan. However, individual inquiries you make yourself do not count negatively against you. If you are curious as to the contents of your credit file, making an inquiry will not make a difference in the outcome of your credit score.

 Fact #36: Too many credit inquiries by creditors over a short period of time are viewed negatively.

Optional message

This final section of the credit report is a place where you can leave a short personal message. This message can help to explain any special circumstances in your credit file. If you choose to take advantage of this credit report section it is important to be brief. You are only allowed a limited number of words.

 Fact #37: The optional message section of your credit report must be less than 100 words.

What Is Excluded from Credit Reports?

A credit report is not a complete biography of your life. While there are many facts and figures connected to your financial history, more personal information is not allowed to appear anywhere on your report.

Fact #38: Purchases made by cash or check do not appear on your credit report.

The following items are not included on your report:

- Gender

- Race

- Religion

- Political affiliation

Other notable exemptions are checking and savings account information, purchases made by cash or check, and credit scores. Your score will be determined based on stats in your report. Credit scores are not part of the report. They are purchased separately as an individual score or bundled together with a copy of the report.

Fact #39: Even though credit scores are calculated from credit report information, they are not included on a credit report.

While this information is barred from appearing on a credit report, that doesn't mean that a company can't find out personal information based on your history. For example, your employment history, address history, and names of companies that appear on your report could be clues to more personal information about you.

If a creditor named Magnolia Lane Psychiatric appears on your report, an institution considering giving you a line of credit might assume you are receiving some type of mental health care. While there are laws preventing discrimination associated with credit report findings, it is important to know that lending institutions can discover a lot about you from the bread crumbs you leave behind.

Check your credit reports to make sure they are accurate. Under the Fair and Accurate Credit Transactions Act of 2003, consumers are allowed to request one free copy of their credit reports annually from all three credit bureaus.

If you notice any billing errors with your creditors, inform them immediately. These errors can normally be corrected. The Fair Credit Billing Act contains a law allowing consumers to withhold payments for billing errors while the creditor investigates the error. The creditor must be notified within 60 days of the date of the statement with the billing error. The creditor has 90 days to complete the investigation.

—JeFreda Brown, MBA, business consultant and CEO of Goshen Business Group, LLC

The Credit Report Life Cycle

Your credit report is constantly evolving. Accounts, collections, judgments, and bankruptcies all have a limited amount of time they are included in your report. Most states have laws that establish the amount of time certain report entries can remain visible. This helps guarantee that even with a complicated past filled with negative credit consequences, over time you can still make the changes necessary to get back on solid financial ground.

 Fact #40: Except in California and New York, credit report entries have a lifespan of seven or ten years.

CHAPTER 3

Credit Scoring Models

After reading over your credit report, you might wonder why you have to then pay a credit-reporting agency to calculate your credit score. Why can't you just do it yourself? The truth is it takes more than a copy of your credit report and a calculator to find your credit score. Each agency uses their own unique scoring model to find your personal credit score. If you go to three different agencies, you could purchase three totally different scores.

In order for a credit-reporting agency to arrive at a credit score, they use a credit scoring model. A credit scoring model is a complex set of algorithms and calculations that process the information from your credit report and deliver a three digit score as the result.

The algorithms take the information already contained in your report. Your credit history, timeliness of payments, outstanding debts, and new credit requests are processed along with personal information you provide on your credit application.

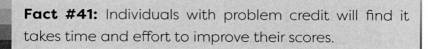

Fact #41: Individuals with problem credit will find it takes time and effort to improve their scores.

By using a combination of paying down debt and disputing any negative information in your credit report, over time you will see an improvement in your individual score.

FICO—The King of Credit Scores

There are many different credit scoring models that exist for lenders to choose from, but there is only one they trust: the FICO score. The FICO score is the all-knowing and all-powerful king of credit scores. Banks and credit card companies use the FICO score as a way to determine credit worthiness and interest rates.

Credit reporting agencies will offer other credit scoring models to lenders, but they never use them. They count on the FICO. Since even FICO scores can vary by which agency is providing them, lenders will often average the scores together and use that as their basis for making an offer to you.

The FICO score is not only limited to banks and credit card companies. As an individual, you can obtain a FICO score yourself. FICO has enacted changes to their policies in recent years making it easier to obtain an official score.

Fact #42: Since 2013, individuals can access their free FICO score through the FICO Score Open Access Program.

Your FICO score is like a basketball team. There are five players. Each player can only score so many points per game, so you want to put out the best team possible. You have two guards: One is named Payment History and the other is Amounts Owed. You also have two forwards: Length of Credit History and Types of Credit Used. Finally, you have your center: we'll call him New Credit.

Now that everyone is warmed up, let's get on the court and meet the team!

Payment history

The first player contributing to your FICO score is Payment History. This member of your team is definitely the MVP. Payment History is going to be responsible for putting up the most FICO score baskets. It is a good thing to have some sort of credit payment history. If you are making your payments on time, it shows that you are a responsible consumer.

Fact #43: Having too many credit accounts may have a negative impact on your credit score.

Accounts in your payment history can be both open and closed. Because it is your credit past, even inactive accounts are included. You'll want to keep an eye on the overall number of accounts you have. Keeping an eye on your open accounts and their balances can help better regulate your credit score. Your payment history also details if you pay only the minimum balance due, more than the minimum balance due, or the full amount each month.

The payment history portion of your FICO score is determined by the following:

- Number of accounts

- Negative public records

- Number of unpaid accounts

- Late payments

The younger you are, the less payment history you have to offer. A negative record will be more obvious on such a short credit report. The older you are, the more lengthy your payment history, so a negative record does not stick out as much.

Amounts owed

Your second best player and contributor to your FICO score is Amounts Owed. This section helps calculate your debt-to-credit ratio. Debt-to-credit ratio is a major indicator of what your overall credit budget should be.

Credit score calculation focuses on four parts of your Amounts Owed:

- How much is owed and what types of accounts

- How much available credit is being used

- Payment consistency

- Number of zero account balances

Fact #44: Your debt-to-credit ratio is how much you owe versus how much you are allowed to borrow.

These two backcourt dynamos provide more than half of your FICO score points. If you are looking to improve your credit score, you will be rewarded if you make sure these two sections are in tip-top playing condition.

Length of credit history

While Length of Credit History is an important member of our team, it doesn't put up nearly the points of our previous two players. The length of time that you have credit established still plays a role in your credit score.

No credit history is like handing in a blank job application. You may tell them you can work hard, but with no evidence to back up your claims, few bosses will be calling you in for an interview. Even if you are always making your payments on time or paying the full balance, your score can still take a hit because there isn't enough evidence of a strong credit background.

Fact #45: Having no credit history will have a negative impact on one's credit score.

Opening too many credit card accounts too quickly is a sign of financial immaturity. Credit score calculation focuses on three parts of your Length of Credit History:

- Total length of time tracked by the credit report

- Length of time since accounts were opened

- Length of time since the last activity

Types of credit

The type of credit that you accumulate is also a factor in determining your credit score. Our Types of Credit player is still a strong contributor to our team.

Some types of credit are considered more risky than others. A credit report consisting of all credit card loans could lower your score. A credit report with a combination of credit cards and a home mortgage could potentially raise your score because it demonstrates a level of credit stability.

Fact #46: Not all types of credit are equal in the eyes of creditors or the credit bureaus.

Credit score calculation focuses on two parts of your Types of Credit:

- Total number of accounts

- Types of accounts

New credit

The final member of our team roster, New Credit, is the last piece of the FICO score puzzle. Each time you apply for a credit card or other line of credit, an inquiry is added to your credit report.

Inquiries are a part of everyone's credit report. The problems begin to arise when there are too many inquiries made in a short period of time. Sometimes a credit card company will make an inquiry on your behalf.

Fact #47: Only inquiries on a credit report made by businesses count towards your credit score.

If you open too many credit card accounts too quickly, your credit score will take a sharp decline. With no payment history or varying types of credit, your overall score will drop.

After a history of past credit problems, opening new accounts is actually encouraged. By opening new accounts and making payments in a timely manner, your credit score will start to trend upward.

Credit score calculation focuses on five parts of your New Credit:

- New accounts vs. total number of accounts

- Number of recent credit inquiries

- Length of time since most recent inquiry

- Re-establishing a positive credit history after credit problems

- Attempts to open numerous new accounts

FICO for Newbies

In the last section you learned the important role credit history plays in calculating your FICO score. But, what if you want a credit score and you have no history?

Luckily, FICO developed a scoring model for individuals who wouldn't otherwise have a FICO score.

The FICO expansion score is used to predict risk for consumers who do not have a credit history. It is perfect for young people who have yet to develop a credit history, or new U.S. citizens. While many people in this country have established lines of credit in their names, there is still a large segment of the population who have yet to fill out an application.

Fact #48: It is estimated that about 50 million citizens fall into the category of individuals with little or no credit history.

Your first credit card will most likely carry a high interest rate due to your lack of a credit history. The FICO expansion score is designed to help credit card companies assess risk and lessen these costly interest rates. Your expansion score is calculated by gaining access to non-credit data files, like utility bills or alternative payment histories.

VantageScore—The Prince of Credit Scoring Models

In the credit scoring model castle, the FICO score is the king in the high tower. While he looms over his kingdom, there is another member of the scoring model royal family . . . the VantageScore model. The VantageScore scoring model is like the Prince. He isn't as powerful or well respected as the FICO, but still plays a strong role in the credit-reporting kingdom.

 Fact #49: The VantageScore scoring model focuses on key areas of your credit history.

Just as the FICO scoring model examines specific sections of a credit report, the VantageScore model examines six key parts:

1. Payment history

2. Use

3. Balances

4. Depth of credit

5. Recent credit

6. Available credit

Let's take a closer look at what goes into the making of the VantageScore.

Payment history

The biggest piece of the VantageScore model is payment history. It takes an in-depth look at your payments and when you make them. It penalizes you for late payments and rewards you for payments made on time.

Use

This section details the amount of available credit you have and how much of it you are using at a given time. Using a large amount of your available credit is a strong risk indicator.

Balances

By not paying off your accounts in full, your credit history starts to carry various account balances. This section details those balances, both current and delinquent.

Depth of credit

This section makes up a smaller piece of your total VantageScore. It looks at the length of your credit history as well as the types of credit you are holding.

Recent credit

This section chronicles all recently opened accounts and new credit inquiries.

Available credit

This final section is similar to Use. It covers all of your available credit, both used and unused.

Fact #50: The VantageScore scale ranges from 501 to 990 points.

The VantageScore scoring model, while not as popular as the FICO, is still widely used.

Other Types of Scoring Models

The FICO and the VantageScore are not the only scoring models used. Creditors use predictive scoring models to anticipate how a consumer will behave if given a line of credit. The types of predictive scoring models include behavior, bankruptcy, profitability, and insurance scoring.

Behavior scoring

Behavior scoring compares your credit file and payment history against other consumers in a credit card company's database. It is used to generate statistics about payment tardiness.

Behavior scoring isolates the following:

- Late payments

- Credit limits

- Cash advances

It is very common and used by more than half of all credit card companies. Your behavior score can help a credit card company decide if they should increase your credit limit. They also use the score as a deciding factor on giving you an account in the first place.

> **Fact #51:** Behavior scoring is used to determine which customers are most likely to pay their bills on time.

Bankruptcy scoring

Much like the FICO score and VantageScore, bankruptcy scoring is performed by credit reporting agencies and given to credit card companies.

Bankruptcy scoring is different from some of the other scoring models. If your employment history reads like a novel, a card company will have some concerns about your job stability.

It looks at past positions held, the type of job you currently have, and how long you have been employed there. Even if you pay your bills on time, you could still be considered a risk for bankruptcy by a credit card company, if you haven't held your job for very long, or if your job seems to have no opportunity for advancement.

Fact #52: Bankruptcy scoring models focus less on your payment history and credit usage and more on your employment history.

Profitability scoring

While credit card companies and banks certainly help you with your financial growth, it is important to remember that they are still businesses. The goal of any business is to make money. The profitability scoring model looks for people who spend and spend often.

Fact #53: The profitability scoring model helps identify consumers who will assist a credit card company in generating the most profit.

If you own a credit card, but don't use it, you are not generating any revenue for the company. The profitability scoring model helps identify card users who will make a variety of purchases and carry balances on their cards. These customers are vital to a credit card company's success, because the company's profit comes directly from the interest rates imposed on their customers. If customers don't use their credit, or pay off their cards immediately, then interest can't be charged, and the company can't profit.

Insurance scoring

Insurance companies use their own type of scoring model to decide whether to provide or deny insurance to an individual. The insurance scoring model is typically used by auto and homeowner insurance companies.

The insurance score can be used to decide if you are eligible for discounts or if you should be denied coverage altogether. If a company chooses to deny coverage they need to be clear on what grounds they are basing the decision.

Fact #54: In some states, it is illegal for insurance companies to deny coverage based on scores from insurance scoring models.

Credit Risks

Just because you have a low credit score, doesn't mean you will be rejected for every line of credit you apply for. Remember, credit card companies and banks are in the business of making money. If they constantly rejected individuals because of low credit scores, they would be abandoning a profitable stream of income.

If you fall into the lower range of credit scores, you will be considered a high credit risk. You will be forced to pay higher interest rates and other fees.

Most people fall under the category of normal credit risk. You are considered to have normal credit risk if any of the following apply to you:

- You have a total of 11 accounts

- You have a credit card balance of less than $1,000

- You have a credit card or loan from the same source for 13 years

These criteria help you maintain your status in the normal credit risk category.

Some actions can have you fall out of this category rather quickly. Missing a payment can abruptly lower your score. A bankruptcy may reduce a score by 200 or more points.

One place you don't want to find yourself is in the category of high credit risk. You are considered to have high credit risk if any of the following apply to you:

- You have a credit history less than two years old

- You have an account closed due to default

- You have payments due that are more than 90 days late

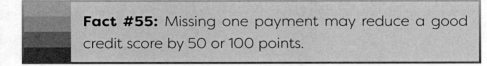

Fact #55: Missing one payment may reduce a good credit score by 50 or 100 points.

The more risk you carry, the higher the interest rate your account will carry. If you find yourself in possession of a credit card with a high interest rate, it is important to try and carry little or no balance on that card. It will help you save money and raise your credit score in the process.

CHAPTER 4

Building Credit

B uilding a good credit history is a lot like building a house. You want to make sure you have a strong foundation so the rest of the house won't collapse. Good credit history is built on a solid payment history. Making payments on time is a necessary step in building or maintaining a strong credit score. Unpaid bills can lead to negative entries on your credit report and cause your financial dream house to come crashing down.

> Building credit is something that takes time. Trying to do it quickly can cause problems. Just because different types of credit are available, it does not mean all of them are right for you. There are some credit cards that require applicants to pay a fee, which they call a processing fee, in order to obtain a credit card. Then, they charge an annual fee to the card. By the time you receive the card, there is only a small amount of money available.
>
> —JeFreda Brown, MBA, business consultant and CEO of Goshen Business Group, LLC

Credit-Building Accounts

When you are starting out, your first step in building credit is to open a savings account or checking account, or both. This step in your financial life usually coincides with your first job. You'll need a place to deposit those first paychecks and a bank account is an excellent destination for your hard-earned money.

Your next step after building up some savings and getting some banking history entries on your credit report is to open a credit card. Your first credit card will probably carry a hefty interest rate due to your lack of credit history. In these early months it is important to make payments early and often.

Fact #56: Credit card companies are allowed to pre-screen names and make pre-approved offers to consumers who pass the screening.

Many "pre-approved" credit offers will stuff your mailbox during your early days of building credit. These offers may seem too good to be true, and that's because they are. After you apply for the card, a more intense credit screening occurs which often results in a less-than-stellar offer.

In this chapter, you'll learn about the different types of credit accounts available to you. There are many pros and cons to each and you'll gain a better idea as to which best suits you as a consumer.

Remember to choose wisely; these early decisions will determine the quality of your credit mansion's foundation.

Bank accounts

A picture of your piggy bank is not going to make a credit card company trust you. Having a savings or checking account is a great way to demonstrate to lenders that you have a way to pay your bills.

The best way to start building your credit is to open a bank account. Opening both a savings and a checking account is best. This helps create stability. It also shows that you are able to handle your finances. Establishing a good relationship with your banker is key. The banker can then help you open a credit card account. I would recommend obtaining a credit card from the bank or credit union you have accounts with. I would also recommend just starting with one credit card.

—JeFreda Brown, MBA, business consultant and
CEO of Goshen Business Group, LLC

Opening a checking or savings account is an easy process. Your parents can even open a joint account for you to help you get started on the right foot. Once you are employed, check to see if your employer offers a direct deposit program. This way, you don't have to worry about taking a paper check to your bank.

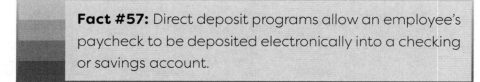

Fact #57: Direct deposit programs allow an employee's paycheck to be deposited electronically into a checking or savings account.

Credit cards

When you think of the word "credit," a credit card is usually the image that comes to mind. Those little plastic rectangles with fun colors and logos help fill the empty spaces in your wallet. A card company will give you a maximum amount of money you are allowed to spend in a given month. This amount is called your credit limit.

Fact #58: Credit cards allow consumers to carry a balance from month to month.

As long as you pay the minimum monthly payment and don't exceed your credit limit, you will build a stronger credit history each month. Paying more than your minimum can help lower your account balance more quickly, helping you save more for your future.

If trying to build a stronger credit background, be sure to keep your balance far lower than your maximum credit limit.

> Credit cards are not bad. It is irresponsible use of the cards that is the root of the problem. If you can get a credit card from a bank or credit union to start building your credit, don't be surprised if your interest rate is extremely high. That is because the lender doesn't know how you will handle the borrowed money. Be sure that you do not spend more with the card than you can pay off when the bill comes. Paying your credit card bill on time will help avoid paying interest. Remember, your credit card is not an emergency fund. Use it for small purchases here and there to help build a solid credit score.
>
> —Amber Berry, certified financial education instructor and certified money coach

Charge cards

While not as popular, an alternative to credit cards are called charge cards. A charge card works just like a credit card, except the balance must be paid in full at the end of each month.

If you fail to make a monthly payment on a charge card, the company can end your access to the account. Depending on your financial standing, a charge card can be a high-risk/high-reward situation.

Fact #59: Charge cards can help build your credit history quickly.

If you make timely payments on a charge card, you will start to see more offers for credit cards.

Specialty credit cards

Some companies will offer a credit card specific to their business. You've probably seen them. They usually carry the logo and company colors. These cards are usually limited to purchases on specific types of goods, usually those offered by the card issuer. Specialty card issuers are usually involved in the retail and travel industry.

Like other credit and charge cards, as long as payments are made on time and an established credit limit is not exceeded, specialty credit cards will help build good credit.

Fact #60: Airlines, gas stations, hotels, and retail stores are all examples of companies that supply specialty credit cards.

Secured credit cards

Rebuilding your credit history after a financial collapse of bankruptcy can be a challenge. Fortunately, secured credit cards can help you. A secured credit card is a credit account linked to a savings account in a bank. It works just like any other credit card, but the credit limit is tied to the amount of funds available in your savings account.

Secured credit cards routinely carry high interest rates and a variety of extra fees. However, if you're looking to repair your credit score, they offer a path to a higher rating. Failure to make payments does not mean the credit card company will take your money from your savings account. The card company will follow a late payment policy just like any other regular credit card. Funds would only be taken as a last resort.

Fact #61: Continued success with a secured credit card can lead to a card company converting you to an unsecured card.

Over time, a card company may track your progress and take notice of your timely payments. Some companies may even make you an offer for a new line of unsecured credit. Everyone is different. For some consumers this process can take months, for others it can take years. It all depends on your personal financial habits.

Prepaid credit cards

Some credit cards are available without the need for a credit history check. These prepaid credit cards are loaded with funds at the time of purchase. Once the amount funded to the card is used up, the card can be reloaded with additional funds, or it can be closed.

If you decide to use prepaid credit cards to help build a credit history, be sure to check that the company who supplies the card reports your activity to credit agencies. It would be a shame for all of your hard work to go unnoticed.

Fact #62: Prepaid credit cards allow for purchases up to the amount prepaid for the card.

Installment accounts

When you make the decision to either buy a car or a home, you will become familiar with installment accounts. Installment accounts are a big part in the financing of major purchases. The most common examples of installment accounts include auto loans and home mortgages.

Fact #63: Installment accounts allow you to borrow a specific amount of money and pay it back with interest over time.

As long as the terms of the loan agreement are met, these types of accounts can help build your credit. Be careful if a car dealership offers you something called "second chance financing." The salesperson may convince you that it is the deal of a lifetime, but upon closer inspection of the fine print, it is anything but. These types of loans are conducted through the dealership and not a bank. They can carry huge interest rates and additional fees.

Major purchases

In your life, you will make many big-ticket purchases. These items or experiences will carry such a hefty price tag that unless you're independently wealthy, you will certainly need to take out a loan. The good news is that making these large purchases by taking out a corresponding loan will help you build a better credit score.

Major purchases are items that exceed the credit limit on most cards, are too big to carry home, and would require more cash than most people carry in their wallets. The loans associated with these expenses differ as well. Vehicle, home, and student loans all contain their own set of specifications for how the loan is structured. Let's take a look at a few below.

 Fact #64: Major purchases include things like a home, a car, furniture, or even a college education.

Car loans

After you pass your driver's test, you'll put your focus towards a car. If you aren't fortunate enough to borrow your parent's or an older sibling's ride, you'll need to buy a car.

Spending time at a car dealership will most likely leave you with a severe case of sticker shock. Even used cars will probably be out of your price range. How will you ever be able to afford a car with only the pay from your summer lifeguarding gig, or flipping burgers at a local fast food joint?

The answer is by taking out a loan. Most car dealerships will offer some sort of financing options. Remember, not even people who drive luxury cars walked into a dealership with over $100,000 in cash. Everyone uses loans to help afford these major purchases.

 Fact #65: Vehicle leases usually require little or no down payment.

Your first decision in the loan process is to decide whether to buy or lease your vehicle. A lease is like a rental agreement. The advantage of a lease is there is little or no upfront cost. A big disadvantage is they are often more costly. If you decide to buy a car, you will first decide how much money to use as a down payment. After that, you will structure a payment schedule for the remaining amount. Car loans are usually spread out over two to five years.

No matter which you choose, it is important to examine all of your available options. Making on-time auto payments is another way to help build a strong credit reputation.

Home loans

If you thought buying your first car was expensive, just wait until you enter the world of home ownership. Depending on the type of home you are looking to buy and where it is located, the price tag of a new house can quickly jump into the hundreds of thousands of dollars.

Just like a car, very few people can buy a home outright. To ease the burden and financial hardships of home ownership, lending institutions will offer a home loan called a mortgage. A mortgage is loan agreement made to help a buyer purchase a home. Much like a car loan, a down payment is made initially, followed by monthly payments over a specific period of time.

Fact #66: Most mortgage loans are spread out over 15 or 30 years.

Student loans

Even if a new car or home is not in your immediate future, a college education will most likely be in your plans. The cost of a four-year degree program at a college or university far exceeds a new car, and in some cases, more than a new house.

To help pay for college, you may have to take out student loans. These loans help you pay for college while you are in attendance and pay them back after you graduate. Just like car and home loans, student loans can carry high interest rates and fees.

Fact #67: Student loans are reported to credit reporting agencies and included in credit files.

Paying back your student loans after college can help improve your credit history. If you choose to pay off your loans in one big payment, you'll have a great financial weight off your shoulders, but your rating won't improve because you'll lack a payment history demonstrating good habits. (The same is true for a car loan or mortgage.) If you fail to pay back student loans after college, you will suffer the same consequences as failing to make other types of loan payments. Even after graduation, this information will still appear in your credit file.

After college, you may attempt to consolidate your loans into one payment. This will help you have more time to pay your loans off and you can usually find a better interest rate as well.

Accounts That Won't Help

No one wants to do more work than needed. Imagine writing an essay for school. You stay up all night trying to cram in a few more pages, only to find out the next day it only needed to be two pages long.

It is very important for you to understand the types of accounts that won't impact your credit history. You don't want to be spending money, time, and resources trying to improve an account that doesn't impact your score.

Some of these accounts are reported to credit reporting agencies, but won't affect your file. They may even carry additional fees that will cost you more money but deliver no credit benefits.

Passport loans

A passport loan has nothing to do with international travel. It is not a loan to be able to afford a passport or finance a passport. A passport loan is a loan against money you already have in a bank account. You take out the loan and then make quick payments using money you already have. It demonstrates responsibility to the credit reporting agency.

One problem with passport loans is they are not as respected in the industry as a credit card. You would be better off finding another type of account to help rebuild your credit history.

Fact #68: Passport loans are often not reported to credit reporting agencies.

Should you choose to go this route, it is important to pick a passport loan that will be reported and make sure your payments are made on time.

Finance company loans

You've probably seen late night TV commercials for companies claiming to give loans to people with bad credit or no credit. There is usually a zany spokesperson screaming at the top of their lungs. If these companies are so great, wouldn't everyone use them?

Fact #69: The reputation of the company giving you a loan can also affect your credit.

These finance companies usually have lousy reputations and credit reporting agencies will not value their reports. They are also riddled with sky-high interest rates and loads of extra fees and charges.

You'd be better off seeking out a more traditional loan from an established bank or credit card company. Don't fall victim to their creative advertising; make sure your credit file is working in your favor.

One-time references

The size of the company making a claim about your credit history affects you. Smaller, less established companies that make one-time reports to credit reporting agencies often have little effect on your rating.

Most credit reporting agencies will not research these companies or put any extra effort into examining their business. Reporting agencies place greater emphasis on payment patterns and not one-time references.

You would hope that any positive evidence of good credit would benefit your credit history, but in the case of these one-time references, credit reporting agencies are not going to contact them for a review.

Fact #70: Credit card companies base their loan decisions on payments made over time.

Catalog cards

A catalog card is a credit card that is issued along with a catalog. The card may only be used to order items found within the pages of the catalog. They are not very popular among consumers and the products offered in the catalogs are usually things like used electronics or cheap jewelry.

Fact #71: Catalog cards are often referred to as "paper cards."

There is usually a high fee associated with just obtaining the card. The catalog card industry is ripe with fraud. Credit reporting agencies will rarely consider reports from these companies. Be careful if you choose to explore this seldom-used credit option.

Rent-to-owns

A rent-to-own account is exactly what it sounds like. You pay to borrow a product or goods, and over time you will pay off the debt and own the item. Many states do not monitor rent-to-own accounts and they are not reported to credit agencies.

This type of account usually preys on low-income consumers. The companies involved with the loan are hopeful that the consumer won't be able to make payments, and that they will surrender the money already paid towards the product. This loan will do nothing to help your credit report.

The biggest drawback to this type of loan is the interest rate. They are usually very high and taking the loan is not a wise business decision.

> **Fact #72:** Rent-to-own accounts can carry interest rates as high as 200 percent.

Cosigning

When starting out with little or no credit history, you will probably turn to your parents for help. A parent can act as a cosigner, easing the process in getting a credit card or other type of loan account in your name.

A cosigner is a third party to a loan who guarantees that the loan gets repaid. Think of it like a backup quarterback in football. If your starter can't get the job done, your backup, or cosigner, will take the field and score the winning drive.

The credit history on accounts where a cosigner is attached is present in both parties' credit files. As long as the accounts are in good standing, a cosigned loan can help everyone involved.

A disadvantage of having a cosigner is your credit behavior can have an effect on their credit history. If you don't pay your bills and your account enters the delinquency phase, the credit card company will expect your cosigner to pay the balance. It may take up to 60 days for your cosigner to be notified of your late payments. This credit failure can negatively impact your cosigner's credit score more than your own.

 Fact #73: A cosigned loan can help improve both parties' credit standing with a credit reporting agency, as long as adequate payments are made regularly.

In your future, you may be a cosigner for your own children or another family member. Being a cosigner on too many accounts in addition to your own debt can place you in a higher credit risk category. While helping out someone in need is a good thing, being a cosigning superhero could hurt you in the end.

Authorized Use

Some credit cards allow for more than one user on an account. This occurs most often among families. Your parents may authorize you and your siblings to use a credit card in their name.

The main advantage of Authorized Use is it helps build credit among children in a family. When you are attached to a credit account, the credit history associated with the account gets placed in your credit file. As your parents make payments on time, your credit history gets a bump in the right direction.

 Fact #74: Families most often practice Authorized Use to help boost one another's credit rating.

The only danger regarding Authorized Use would be if your parents failed to make payments or were late with many payments in a row. Since the credit history from the card is synced to both of your accounts, this bad credit behavior would be part of your credit file as well.

Third Party Accounts

Depending on where you live, you could be responsible for your spouse's account. Third party accounts are basically forced cosigning accounts. In certain community property states, your spouse is responsible for your debts and vice-versa.

Out of the fifty U.S. states, only nine honor community property laws. If you live in one of these states, it makes sense to cosign for each other's credit cards. Any positive credit outcomes will be transferred to the other.

> **Fact #75:** The nine community property states are Arizona, California, Idaho, Louisiana, Nevada, New Mexico, Texas, Washington, and Wisconsin.

Expand and Manage Credit Accounts

On your financial journey, special circumstances may arise in your credit lifestyle. You might get married. You might get divorced. Maybe you'll go to college or join the military. No matter what specific situation arises, you'll have to adapt your credit practices to help you meet your goals.

Marriage

For women, the road to credit freedom has been a rocky one. There was a time when a woman's individual credit was canceled as soon as she was married. She would be forced to cosign with her husband's accounts. Credit card companies could also ask about a woman's future family plans, inquiring about how many children she was planning to have.

Thanks to the Equal Credit Opportunity Act (ECOA), women no longer have to deal with such shenanigans. They are entitled to the same credit freedoms as men regardless of their marital status.

Fact #76: The Equal Credit Opportunity Act (ECOA) established that women were entitled to credit in their own names if they met the criteria.

Once married, your credit status is evaluated differently. You are encouraged to not share all accounts. It is important to have both jointly held and individual credit card accounts. If you decide to split up, all of your credit will not be tied to one individual.

The ECOA allows you to use your birth name, married name, or a combination of both. Should you decide to change your name, be sure to contact your credit card companies to avoid any reporting confusion in your credit file.

Divorce

On your wedding day, you probably won't be thinking about getting a divorce. You definitely won't be thinking about divorce and your credit rating.

When a marriage ends in divorce, any joint credit accounts still appear in credit files. If a spouse was only considered an authorized user, they have no responsibility for repaying any debts on the account.

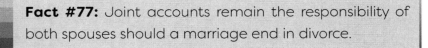

Fact #77: Joint accounts remain the responsibility of both spouses should a marriage end in divorce.

The accompanying financial headaches that follow most divorces can be very aggravating. During divorce proceedings, if one spouse attempts to damage another's credit rating by not paying debts, there are laws and statutes protecting the rights of the other.

Separating joint credit accounts is no easy feat, but any good divorce lawyer will help ease the burden during this very difficult time.

Widows

If you've ever been to a funeral, you've probably overheard family members discussing financial matters. A death can be a stressful time for a family. Funeral expenses are bad enough, but couple that with resolving credit issues and you have a perfect storm of credit stress.

If a death occurs in a marriage, the surviving spouse is not responsible for debts in the name of the deceased. They are only responsible for any joint account debts. Sometimes a credit company will attempt to settle debts from a deceased individual but only in extreme cases.

Credit reporting agencies should be notified of a death and be provided with a death certificate as proof. This will help ensure that credit mailing offers are stopped and the likelihood of any identity theft issues is diminished.

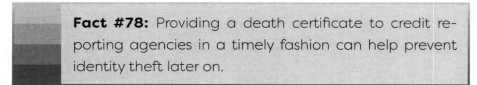

Fact #78: Providing a death certificate to credit reporting agencies in a timely fashion can help prevent identity theft later on.

College

For many students, college is a time of independence. For the first time in your young life, you are on your own. This is an attractive situation for credit card companies who often target college campuses to acquire a new customer base.

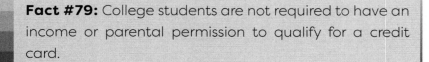

Fact #79: College students are not required to have an income or parental permission to qualify for a credit card.

During college, in some situations, all you'll have to do is sign on the dotted line, and a credit card will be mailed to you. Credit card companies are optimistic that you'll use your card often and continue to use it well after graduation.

The card companies don't consider you a risk, because they assume if you fall behind on your payments, your parents will be there to help you. It is probably a good idea to get at least one card during your college experience. Many credit card companies aren't as loose with their offers after you graduate and enter the workforce.

Seniors

Some senior citizens have never had a credit card in their lifetime. They have spent decades using cash and checks for purchases and making an almost daily journey to the local bank. Despite their resistance to change, a senior citizen who opens a credit card account can still gain many benefits.

> **Fact #80:** Credit cards provide safety, convenience, and emergency buying power.

Credit cards, in some instances, are safer than cash or checks. If an elderly man opens his wallet to pay for a gallon of milk at a grocery store revealing a crisp row of $100 bills, he is notifying the public of his wealth. This can invite criminals and other con-artists to possibly take advantage of him. Credit cards offer no insight into a person's bank account. Credit cards provide convenience and are invaluable in an emergency situation.

Military

In addition to college or entering the workforce, another path you may follow after high school is towards a career in the military. While the military offers many benefits, there are some drawbacks with regard to obtaining lines of credit.

Credit card companies have a difficult time assessing credit files of members of the armed forces. Military income is not very high and soldiers are often moving from one base to another.

 Fact #81: Military persons stationed overseas should use their hometown address for credit card applications.

Entrepreneurs

One of the biggest challenges when starting your own business is finding the money to make it happen. You can go to a bank for a loan, but often the requirements and interest rates they offer are too steep.

 **Fact #82:** Bankruptcy law and exemptions can encourage or discourage small business growth, depending on their severity. In the United States, restrictions can vary from state to state.

A great alternative to a loan for starting your business is credit cards. Business credit cards offer easy access to cash in the early stages of building your brand.

There are some challenges to obtaining credit cards for your new business. Not all companies are going to trust your business idea and throw money in your direction. Some lenders may consider it risky. Not naming your company after yourself is one strategy for disassociating your credit history from your future company. They type of company you have can also help with receiving lines of credit.

Immigrants

Even if you are not a resident of the United States, some companies will still offer you a line of credit. It is illegal for a credit card company to discriminate based on ethnicity or race. However, they will take into account whether or not you are a resident of this country.

A company may reject a credit application if they feel it would be too difficult to recover any debts should the consumer leave the country.

Fact #83: Some companies will still provide credit to non-U.S. citizens if they can provide proof of a residence.

Managing Debt

Credit card companies have different ways of measuring how you manage your debt. When you establish a credit card account, it is your responsibility to monitor the account. The credit card company will track your habits and assess if you are taking on too much. The three most common methods for tracking your debt intake are debt-to-income ratio, current ratio calculations, and determining a comfort level.

Debt-to-income ratio

The debt-to-income model compares how much money you make each month to how much money you owe to pay bills. It is basically an in vs. out approach. This ratio looks at your total income and then subtracts away the money you owe for your mortgage, car payment, or credit card bills and calculates your financial stability.

> The debt-to-income ratio is your total monthly debt payments divided by your total monthly gross income. It lets creditors see how capable you are of making monthly debt payments. As a young adult, you most likely have rent and a car note. You may even have a credit card. If your monthly rent is $850, you monthly car payment is $575, and your monthly credit card payment is $50, then your total monthly debt payments are $1,475. If your monthly gross income is $3,500, then your debt-to-income ratio is about 42 percent. This is considered to be a little high. However, many mortgage lenders will allow up to 43 percent.
> —JeFreda Brown, MBA, business consultant and CEO of Goshen Business Group, LLC

 Fact #84: Debt-to-income ratios are calculated on a monthly or annual basis.

Current ratio calculations

While debt-to-income ratio is a useful tool in assessing your level of debt, it isn't perfect. Another model that is better suited for consumers is the current ratio calculation.

This calculation combines your income and the value of other financial holdings versus your debt. Assets include the value of your home or investment and retirement accounts. It factors in the value of these assets and weighs them against the amount of debt you choose to take on. It is also known as liability/asset ratio.

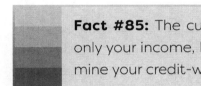

Fact #85: The current ratio calculation examines not only your income, but the value of your assets to determine your credit-worthiness.

Determining a comfort level

This final strategy is one you can do yourself. Rather than have a company comparing your income vs. debt, you can examine your own credit habits. If you notice that you don't have enough money to make payments each month, you need to seek help or develop a better plan for your finances.

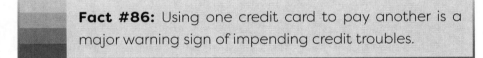

Fact #86: Using one credit card to pay another is a major warning sign of impending credit troubles.

There are many warning signs of credit distress. They include things like denied credit card purchases, ignoring credit statements, or using one credit card to pay another. A common solution for not meeting the income levels needed to pay debts might be to get a second job or work overtime hours at your current job.

CASE STUDY: HOW I FINISHED COLLEGE WITH A 727 CREDIT SCORE

Amber Berry
Certified Financial Education
Instructor and Certified Money Coach
FeelGoodFinances.com
Twitter: @feelgudfinances

When I left home to attend college, I had no credit established. I had never taken out a loan, I had no credit card, nor was I an authorized user on either of my parent's cards. So when I got my first credit card my second year of college, I was starting from ground zero. This meant that the interest rate on the student credit card I had was very high (17 percent and up) and the limit was low ($500). I mostly used it to buy groceries and personal care items if I needed anything before payday. Then I would pay the bill every month. My payment history showed lenders that if I borrowed money, they could count on me to pay them back on time, and this helped me develop a good credit rating. The most important thing for credit card use that I learned early on was that the credit card is not an emergency fund. If the card is only used when an emergency arises, and there is no money set aside to pay it back, it can become quite the challenge to catch up on payments. Carrying balances with interest can be a burden.

My freshman year of college was the most expensive year because I lived on-campus in the dorms. Before moving away for college, I was able to earn enough scholarships and grants to cover the entire year. Focusing on alternative ways to pay for school with part-time work, grants, fee-waivers, and scholarships instead of student loans has made all the difference. Scholarships aren't just for honor roll students. There is a wide variety of scholarships available for athletes, creative arts, and more. It's worth investigating to see what opportunities are out there to help with avoiding the accumulation of excessive student loan debt.

Overall, by the time I finished college, there were several things that I had done to build a solid credit score. I financed a car and religiously submitted on-time payments, I used my credit card responsibly, and I always paid my bills on time. Paying bills on time does not directly improve your score, but missed payments can be reported to the credit bureaus and sent to collections if they are far enough past due, so it was vital to have a system for keeping up with all of my commitments. All of these things combined helped me have a credit score of 727 when I finished college.

CHAPTER 5

Repairing Bad Credit

f you've ever woken up one morning to find an unsightly pimple or blemish on your cheek, you know that wishing it away won't work. You have to put in some work. Wash your face, use a special cleanser; there are many steps you can follow to get your cheeks back to spot-free status.

Your credit history is no different. Wishing for bad credit to just disappear is a hopeless endeavor. You have to be prepared to roll up your sleeves and get to work. Bad credit can cause you to pay more for borrowed money or be denied credit altogether. It can cause missed opportunities, create stress, and put you at a disadvantage with credit company sharks who smell blood in the water.

Bad credit does not always mean failure to pay bills. Your level of borrowing is another strong indicator of credit risk. Even if you are on time with your payments each month, borrowing too much can illuminate a risky pattern in the eyes of credit card companies.

With advances in technology and a move towards an online financial world, the likelihood of identity theft has grown. It is easier than ever for criminals to steal your information and use it for their own purposes, causing the destruction of your credit rating.

If you run into bad credit issues, it doesn't mean you should give up and accept your new reality. There are several steps you can take and many resources to utilize in your fight to repair your credit file.

Consequences of Bad Credit

The credit history highway is filled with various potholes. Navigating and avoiding the potholes is a key part of maintaining good credit standing. However, you may experience a blowout somewhere along the way and find yourself standing on the side of the road.

The stress of dealing with your credit issues can cause mental or relationship problems. There are many factors that could lead to bad credit. Losing your job, a divorce, a serious illness, could all lead to financial hardship. Even after the underlying issue is resolved, the consequences of bad credit can linger into your future.

Higher interest rates

There is a direct relationship between your credit score and the interest rate you pay on your account balances. The higher your credit score, the lower your interest rate. The lower your credit score, the higher your interest rate. A higher interest rate on your account is one of the leading consequences of having a bad credit history.

Even a small difference in your credit score could increase the interest rate you pay on your account. Interest rates are one of the leading ways credit card companies make a profit. It is no wonder that they will look for any reason to raise your rate.

Fact #87: A difference of 100 points in credit scores may triple the interest rate on your account.

Fees

In addition to higher interest rates, another consequence is having to pay additional fees on an account. If you are late with a payment or charge more than your credit limit, the company may add an extra fee to your bill. These fees can add up quickly, forcing you spend more of your hard-earned money to pay down your debt.

Fact #88: Some credit card companies may waive added fees if contacted directly and a plan is set up to settle any missed payments.

If you notice a rise in additional fees appearing on your monthly statements, you should take action immediately.

Sub-prime loans

Getting a mortgage for a home is no walk in the park. There are many credit check hoops you must jump through before you can sign on the dotted line. If you are experiencing a period of bad credit, the type of loan you qualify for may be risky.

If the mortgage lender considers you a high credit risk you may be offered what is called a sub-prime loan. A sub-prime loan is offered at a much higher interest rate than loans offered to someone with a better credit rating.

While you may be thrilled to know you are getting the funds you need to buy your dream home, these interest rates can cause you problems down the road if the value of your home declines or you experience further financial difficulties.

Lost employment opportunities

If you are up for a promotion at your job, it's possible your boss could take a look at your credit report. Employers often investigate employee's credit history to get a sense of their financial practices.

If your boss sees a long list of late payments or outstanding debts, they may think twice about offering you a raise or a better position in the workplace. Bosses have no time for workers who don't perform. Employers want to keep responsible leaders in their workplace environments.

> **Fact #89:** The link between high stress and poor health is well-known. If you are stressed out about your finances, you're more likely to experience negative physical effects that could cause you to be less focused at work, or cause you to miss more work days.

Higher insurance costs

"If you are experiencing a period of bad credit, you are more likely to have an accident. Bad credit causes financial stress and that can lead to a lack of focus." These are commonly held beliefs of some major insurance companies. These institutions can use credit scores as the basis for increasing your monthly bill or denying you insurance entirely.

Is this even legal? The U.S. government is constantly investigating the practices of insurance companies. There have been numerous attempts to pass legislation to limit their levels of discrimination.

> **Fact #90:** Some states have established laws restricting the use of credit scores in determining insurance costs.

Relationship problems

The final consequence of bad credit is the possibility of relationship problems. Couples have a hard time discussing their finances without getting emotional. If you and your partner are constantly in disagreement over how to handle your finances, you should seek some guidance before things get worse.

Applying for Credit

One of the greatest freedoms you have as an American citizen is the right to free speech. You can voice your opinion by writing a blog, performing a song on a stage, or creating a stunning piece of visual art. You have the right to share your message. However, not everyone has to read your words, hear your music, or view your painting.

Credit card companies have to allow you to apply for a card. You have the right to fill out an application and follow the submission guidelines along with everyone else. However, the card company does not have to approve your application. After reviewing your information, they will make a decision on whether or not to offer you a line of credit.

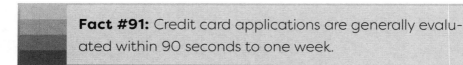

Fact #91: Credit card applications are generally evaluated within 90 seconds to one week.

Card companies must inform you if your application has been approved or denied within 30 days. Most companies will deliver a decision very quickly. If weeks pass and you still have received no word, you should contact a customer service representative.

Fact #92: If consumers do not receive a response to a credit card application within 30 days, they should contact the company to inquire on the application status.

Credit rejection

During your childhood, you probably became very familiar with the word "no". Parents and teachers were always there to stop you in your tracks if you were doing something you shouldn't. Credit card companies have their own method of telling you "no". It is called an adverse action letter.

If your credit card application is reviewed and rejected, you will receive an adverse action letter. There are two key pieces of information contained in this letter. It will detail specific reasons as to why your application was rejected and what reporting agency they obtained your credit report from.

Fact #93: An adverse action letter is sent to a consumer if a credit card application is rejected.

The advantage of an adverse action letter is it gives you a chance to contact the reporting agency and view your credit file contents. You may be able to clear up any inaccurate credit information contained in the files.

Credit Repair

Negative credit issues coupled with financial problems can seem unbearable. As the late notices and excess fees start to pile up, you may feel like there is no way out. Credit repair companies offer services that claim to heal your credit illness and get you back into top credit shape.

Credit repair companies are well-known for scamming individuals by making claims that, for a price, they can fix your credit score. Congress has even passed laws establishing how these companies can accept payment from you.

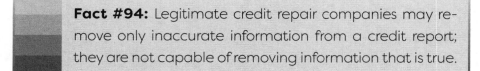

Fact #94: Legitimate credit repair companies may remove only inaccurate information from a credit report; they are not capable of removing information that is true.

The truth is, these credit repair companies use techniques that you can do yourself. A legitimate credit repair company can only remove credit file information that is inaccurate. Any claims that they can remove accurate information like a bankruptcy or unpaid account activity, is a sign of fraud.

Not all credit repair companies are bad. Some provide top-level service and can assist individuals who just don't have the time to focus on their credit file. You should be very careful and research the background of any credit repair companies you may consider hiring. Any promises of a new credit identity should be met with concern. Credit repair success is well within your reach if you work hard and put in the time necessary.

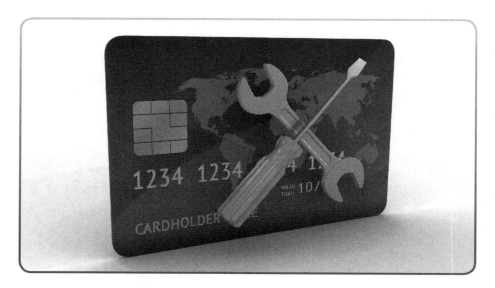

Repairing Your Credit—A Step-by-Step Approach

There are many choices to make when looking to repair your credit rating. Some are more effective than others. It is important not to focus only on one aspect of your credit score. A balanced approach to credit repair will have the best results. If you are looking to improve your rating, you should take on the following tasks.

Give your credit cards a rest

The first step in repairing your credit is to reduce your credit card usage. Having large balances on multiple cards can raise your credit score. You should aim to have your credit card balances below 50 percent of the available credit limit. Having a large debt spread out over many credit cards can also cause credit problems.

> **Fact #95:** Don't open too many credit card accounts in a short period of time.

Opening any new accounts to try and spread out your debt will only drop your credit score more. Pay off any low card balances but don't close the accounts! Closing accounts, especially if they have high credit limits, will make your credit score drop. Paying off the accounts but leaving them open looks good to potential creditors. They can see from your total available credit and low debt that you are a responsible consumer.

If you are tempted to spend on cards with a zero balance, try putting them away somewhere safe, where you can't have immediate access to them, but can use them in a financial emergency.

When you apply for credit, there are five things that creditors look at to determine if you are creditworthy. These five things are called the Five C's of Credit. They are: Character, Capacity, Capital, Collateral, and Condition.

Character is how you have handled your finances. Capacity is how much income you have and how much overall debt you owe. Capital is how much money you have available in savings or liquid assets. Collateral is an asset you own that has value, normally a liquid asset that can be sold for cash. Condition is the current economic condition or environment. Creditors look at the current economic conditions to determine borrowers' ability to repay debts.

—JeFreda Brown, MBA, business consultant and
CEO of Goshen Business Group, LLC

Fix any errors

A bad credit rating can be the result of errors in your credit file. Unless you hire a credit repair company to investigate, it is up to you to examine the contents of your file and fix any errors you find.

The most common errors in credit files include outdated employment history, outdated account balances, duplicate accounts, discharged debts, and mis-merged data.

Fact #96: It is estimated that up to 40 percent of all credit files contain errors.

Each of these errors can result in a lower credit score, preventing you from gaining credit approval. Let's take a closer look at these common credit file mistakes.

Outdated employment history

Part of your credit application includes a section for your employment history. If you change jobs and don't apply for any additional credit accounts, your credit files will only show your past employers. This lack of employment history upkeep can negatively affect your credit limit.

If your last known job was working at a pet store and barely making minimum wage, your credit card company is not going to offer you a high spending limit and competitive interest rate. However, if your most recent job is working for a prestigious law firm and earning over $150,000 annually, your credit card company will feel much more assured in your ability to pay off any borrowed money.

Outdated account balances

Credit card companies will make regular updates to your credit file. The amounts contained in your account balances are always changing as you make payments.

Fact #97: A credit card company's update period can affect the accuracy of your credit report.

The problem arises when your credit files are not updated in a timely manner. If a card company makes monthly updates to reporting agencies, it can take a month or longer before the change is updated in your file. The longer your credit company's update period, the longer your account balance history will remain unchanged.

Duplicate accounts

Another common credit report error is duplicate accounts. This is most often a result of clerical errors or other data entry mistakes. Sometimes accounts have similar numbers and will be entered twice, causing a repeat account filing.

After high school or college you may decide in a change of scenery. A change of address can cause a new account number to be generated. These little mistakes in your file can cause confusion when a lender considers you for a loan. By checking for duplicate accounts, you will help strengthen your credit muscle.

Discharged debts

Hopefully you'll never have to deal with this credit report error. If you declare bankruptcy at any time in your life, the credit card company should report the debt balance as zero and include the appropriate bankruptcy filing. This does not always happen and sometimes the debt owed is still clearly visible on your report.

Fact #98: Discharged debts are often associated with bankruptcy claims.

Mixed-up credit files

If your credit information gets mixed up with another consumer's file, you will both be affected. A common cause of credit file mix-ups is sharing a similar name, address, or other piece of identifying information.

Fact #99: Cases of identity theft often resemble innocent credit file mix-ups.

The only way to amend the file crossover is to contact the credit reporting agency and provide documentation that will explain the situation. Identity theft and fraud can often resemble a simple file mix-up, so it is important to examine the credit file carefully.

Credit report omissions

Remember that your credit file belongs to you. If you feel that something is missing that could help your score, you can take the steps necessary to make sure it is added. Adding additional reports to credit files might help improve your credit rating.

Information added may include loan repayments, salary information, or credit information from a company that doesn't report to credit agencies. While you have the right to make additions to your credit file, it is not a free service. Credit reporting agencies will charge a fee to add the missing items to your file.

Fact #100: Federal law allows consumers to add information to their credit files that they feel will improve their overall rating.

Make a plan

Having a clear plan of action is a necessary step in repairing bad credit. Your credit repair plan should set clear financial goals and outline your spending and saving strategies for the future. Your plan is centered on a budget you create based on your current financial situation. Other parts of your plan include goals, income, expenses, and savings.

Fact #101: A credit repair plan should include a realistic budget based on the amount of income an individual has to work with.

Goals

There are four different types of goals to include in your plan. They are short-term, intermediate-term, long-term, and life goals. Short-term goals are achievable within one year; intermediate-term goals are within five years; and long-term goals are more than five years. Life goals have no time limit and should be more dreams than goals. For example, buying a beach bungalow in Hawaii might be considered a life goal.

Fact #102: Life events may affect your financial goal timeline.

Income

As you gain employment and advance in your career you will probably have more than one source of income. Primary sources of income can include your salary, overtime pay, tips, or royalties. Secondary sources of income are received without much effort and are also known as passive income. This includes money from investments or payments from a rental property.

Make sure you budget according to your net pay and not your gross pay. Net earnings are what you take home after taxes are withheld. Your gross pay is what you make from your job before taxes and other deductions are made.

Fact #103: Gross pay is salary earnings before taxes are withheld.

Expenses

You can think of expenses as the opposite of income. Income is money coming in. Expenses are money going out. Your goal is to maintain a budget where there is more money coming in than there is exiting. It sounds simple enough, but this is often a major financial hurdle for most individuals.

You won't just have one or two expenses. Once you put pen to paper and start making a list, you will see just how many expenses you have. Expenses can include daily, weekly, or monthly payments. It is best to focus on a monthly budget since most expenses will be due on a monthly schedule.

By cutting expenses you can free up extra money in your budget to use towards other needs, like paying off any debt. If you notice your cell phone or cable bill is taking up a significant portion of your budget, changing your plan could help save you a few bucks each month.

Fact #104: It is best to calculate expenses monthly because most are due on that basis.

Savings

If you set up your budget and balance your income and expenses accordingly, you should have some extra money leftover each month. This money is often referred to as savings. Your savings can be used towards retirement, a major purchase, or an emergency fund.

Fact #105: An emergency savings account should include enough money to cover up to six months of expenses.

Talking to your credit card company

Growing up, you were probably taught to talk with a trusted adult in dealing with any challenges you were experiencing. Parents, teachers, coaches all were there to help during your most challenging moments.

A credit card company is not out to punish you. They don't want bad credit problems to ruin your life. They are looking to help you in any way they can so you can pay them back. You should contact your credit card representative as soon as you think there might be a problem making payments.

Fact #106: Credit card companies are more interested in collecting payments than destroying your credit score.

Most companies can be contacted by phone, mail, e-mail, social media, or links on their website. Be positive during your conversation. Remember, they have a mutual interest in helping you keep up with your bills.

Seek credit counseling

Despite your best efforts and taking the actions discussed in this chapter, your credit problems may persist. If you still can't find a way out, you should seek the help of a qualified credit counseling service.

Fact #107: If financial problems are severe, you should seek the help of a credit counselor.

In the next chapter, you will learn more about trustworthy alternatives in the field of credit repair therapy.

CHAPTER 6

Credit Counseling

I f your credit habits are leading you down a path toward financial ruin, one of your final lifelines should be credit counseling. A credit counselor will assist you in managing your debt and help you establish a plan that is unique to your credit situation.

The level of counseling needed may vary from client to client. Credit counseling will help with both short-term and long-term credit issues. If filing for bankruptcy is on your horizon, you'll be required to seek credit counseling before declaring anyway. Taking advantage of these services is a win-win situation.

> **Fact #108:** Bankruptcy proceedings require you to seek credit counseling services before filing.

The Best of the Best

In your search for reputable credit counselors, try and avoid Internet ads or pop-ups urging you to click now and find financial nirvana. There are plenty of less-than-stellar counseling agencies out there. If you are ready to tackle your credit debt head on, you'll want to have the best of the best on your side. Don't just ask someone for a referral. You'll want to seek out a certified organization.

Fact #109: The Council on Accreditation (COA) is the largest third-party accrediting agency for non-profits in the United States.

When you think you've found a good match, make sure that they are an officially licensed and accredited institution. Certain third-party accrediting agencies will certify non-profits and give them their seal of approval. These organizations perform a company-wide audit. They investigate their business practices and company policies before offering to approve their status as an officially licensed credit counseling service.

By seeking a licensed credit counselor, you are helping to protect yourself. You wouldn't visit a doctor who didn't proudly display their medical degree in their office. Don't trust your credit health to a company who won't show you their credentials.

Fact #110: Try and choose a credit counseling service that has been active for at least ten years.

Professionalism

After you choose an accredited and certified counseling service, your next step is to schedule an appointment to meet with them. First impressions go a long way, and if you aren't satisfied with the level of attention you receive, you should seek financial advice elsewhere.

Fact #111: Individuals should inquire about the standards required for credit counseling certification.

These credit counseling services should demonstrate professional behavior. Their employees should treat you with dignity and respect. If you feel your concerns aren't being addressed and they are just trying to rush you in and out the door, you'd be better off in another office.

It is important to remember that these services are non-profits. Their offices won't have the top designer furniture of say, a powerhouse law firm, but it should be clean and respectable. If you visit a credit counselor in the basement of an old washing machine factory, you might want to double check their status as a certified credit counselor.

Fact #112: The level of professionalism exhibited by credit counseling services should match that of other non-profits.

Fees? I Thought This Was a Non-Profit!

If you are speaking with a credit counselor and they want to discuss an initial payment, you should politely thank them for their time and then exit the meeting. A legitimate service will never charge you an up-front fee. It is a sure sign of a scam or a counseling service that has not been certified.

They might try to convince you with some advantages to using their counseling service. They may promise to repay your initial fee after a period of time using their service. The requirements of these deals usually guarantee that repayment never happens.

Remember, non-profit doesn't equal FREE. It just means their business is structured in such a way that all earnings are funneled back into the organization. With most certified credit counseling services, there is still a monthly maintenance fee charged to help defer any office costs for the processing of paperwork or other similar matters.

Your level of need may result in your counselor urging you to set up a debt management plan. Should this be needed, you may be required to pay a plan set-up fee.

Fact # 113: A debt management plan is an ongoing intervention that can take months to complete and usually requires a monthly fee to help manage it.

A majority of clients that utilize credit counselors find that their needs are met through a series of initial meetings. Some require further interventions that will help solve their credit dilemmas. The cost of fees associated with credit counseling varies depending on the institution. It can range from FREE to $50. Monthly debt management plan fees can range from $15 to $50.

These charges are a small price to pay compared to the financial costs of avoiding your debt issues. A credit counseling service is often that last line of defense before a bankruptcy.

Fact #114: It is estimated that about 75 percent of consumers who seek credit counseling find a solution to their financial hurdles.

Counseling Services

An average meeting with a credit counselor is similar to a session with a licensed therapist. There isn't a cozy couch you lie on and you certainly won't delve deep into your past and give details of your current mental health, but you will leave the session feeling a little better about your credit situation.

During a credit counseling session, you will gain insight into your current financial situation and establish a plan to address those issues. You and your counselor will outline goals that you will strive for during the duration of your credit treatment.

An average session will last less than your favorite TV show. There won't be enough time to review individual statements, receipts, or files. However, you will have enough time to ask questions and get advice on the best strategies for your personal credit history.

A credit counselor should be willing to help you arrange new spending habits, set a budget, or start a savings plan.

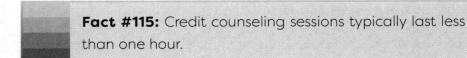

Fact #115: Credit counseling sessions typically last less than one hour.

The most common services performed by credit counseling services include:

- Analysis of your debt owed

- Development of an overview of your personal finances

- Advising you on the steps necessary to reach your goals

- Offering alternatives to your current spending trends

Your first meeting will mostly involve collecting data and other financial disclosures. Income, deductions, and expenses will all be submitted. There will be many questions about your spending habits, so be ready to answer them as best you can.

After examining your records, your counselor will offer suggestions for generating a positive cash flow for your home budget. If no leftover funds exist after reviewing your budget, your counselor will set up a debt management plan for you.

 Fact #116: A positive cash flow means that more money goes into a household than goes out.

Credit counselors are not your parents. They aren't going to yell at you for mismanaging your money. They aren't going to give you a stern lecture about financial discipline. Counseling services will give you options for how to proceed. A good credit counselor will help you find the best plan of action that suits your personal lifestyle and spending habits.

Debt management plans

Credit agreements contain so many details that unless you really read the fine print, you wouldn't be aware of what you were signing. A debt management plan takes advantage of the inner-workings of credit card companies and helps you save money while settling your debts.

 Fact #117: If your credit file shows numerous negative credit entries, a debt management counselor can assist in cleaning it up.

Debt management plans can offer the following advantages:

- Revised monthly payments

- Limited collection calls

- Limited wage garnishments

- Increased payment timeline

- Reduced interest rates

Once a debt management plan is put into action, your credit counselor's role will resemble that of a lawyer. They communicate with your credit card companies on your behalf to explain how you will pay down your debt. The credit card companies would much rather get some money back, so they agree on terms set forth by your credit counselor. This allows you to pay down debt and still have enough money left over to pay monthly expenses.

Most plans last anywhere from two to five years and you'll pay a monthly fee for your counselor to make negotiations and adjustments regarding your payments back to your creditors.

> **Fact #118:** A credit counselor will have more success negotiating with a creditor than an individual trying on their own.

If you and your credit counselor are armed with a strong debt management plan, your financial forecast will improve each month.

In some scenarios, a debt management plan may not be the best course of action. Debt management plans can offer the following disadvantages:

- Difficulty in switching counselors after beginning a plan

- Negative credit file entries

- Limited access to new credit while the plan is in place

But despite these negatives, trying to settle accounts owed without a debt management plan means you'll be expected to pay the total balance on the account, and deal with high interest rates and other hidden fees. A knowledgeable credit counselor who helps author your plan can reduce payments and interest rates, and sometimes get fees waived.

Just like a courtroom lawyer gets excess charges dropped, your debt management team can work miracles for your debt reduction caseload.

Debt settlement plans

Don't confuse management with settlement. Debt settlement plans are not offered by credit counseling agencies. These plans are risky. You'd be better off leaving your money in a casino than entrusting it to a debt settlement agency. Debt settlement companies claim to cure your debt issues by holding your money hostage until a creditor gives up and settles for less than you owe.

It is easy to confuse the two. Be careful of entangling yourself in a messy contract that could destroy your credit score and land you in trouble with the IRS.

Working with one of these companies puts your financial reputation and your money in jeopardy. If you miss just one monthly payment, the debt settlement company could keep all of the money paid so far. Don't be fooled by the claims these companies make.

Fact #119: Even if a debt settlement plan were to succeed, money forgiven would become taxable income for the individual.

Counseling Scams

Advertising plays a major role in credit counseling scams. Companies will make claims that they can't back up. They will use confusing terminology in an attempt to trick customers into subscribing to their services.

 Fact #120: If a company promises to "reduce debt in seconds", they are using false advertising to attract business.

Common phrases used to trick desperate consumers include:

- "Not for profit"

- "Debt-free"

- "Money in your pocket at the end of the month"

- "Erase all your debts and save thousands of dollars"

Don't confuse the phrase "Not for profit" with the term "non-profit". They sound the same but have very different business structures. These are just some of the ways companies attempt to mislead consumers. It is important to do your homework ahead of time to avoid being trapped into an agreement that can't help your credit dilemma.

Fact #121: Credit counseling scams often appeal to a customer's emotions.

Referrals for Counseling Services

Fact #122: Internet searches can be a useful tool in gaining information about potential credit counseling services.

Putting the names of credit counseling services in a hat and drawing one at random is not a good method for picking a company to help you. There are other more calculated ways to choose.

As discussed earlier in the chapter, you'll want to pick an accredited and certified agency to help you with your debt issues. A trusted friend or relative who has experienced similar financial problems could get you started with a few recommendations.

The two most effective search strategies for picking a reputable counseling service involve the Better Business Bureau (BBB) and GuideStar, a web organization that provides information on more than a million non-profits.

Fact #123: The GuideStar website is located at **www.guidestar.org**.

The Better Business Bureau will contain information related to customer complaints, dispute histories, or actions taken against the company. It is a good starting point to see if your counseling candidate is even worth contacting. The GuideStar website provides financial summaries, names of people who sit on a company's board of directors, and tax reports. This web service will help you investigate any misleading company advertisements.

CHAPTER 7

Identity Theft

n high school, your biggest security concern was probably someone stealing your locker combination or copying your exam answers. In the fast-paced world of financial crimes, identity theft is one of the primary factors in credit history disruption.

Identity theft is when someone uses another person's personal information for financial gain. Credit card numbers, birth dates, social security numbers, addresses, and username/passwords are just a few of the weapons in an identity thief's arsenal. Identity theft is a crime. If you use someone's personal information to open a new account or line of credit, you are breaking the law.

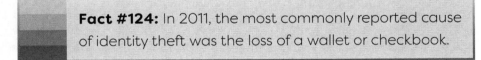

Fact #124: In 2011, the most commonly reported cause of identity theft was the loss of a wallet or checkbook.

So, how do they do it? How do thieves infiltrate and rob you of your personal data? Identity thieves steal from mailboxes, comb through trashcans for discarded receipts, or hack computer systems to get their hands on your precious data. Identity thieves will go to great lengths to get the information they need to commit fraud in your name.

In our current digital age, many financial transactions occur over the Internet. Our current app economy allows you to download mobile applications that provide instant access to your accounts. Despite the vulnerability of these mobile websites, most cases of identity theft do not occur electronically.

The top causes of identity theft are:

- Lost or stolen wallet or checkbook

- Family and friends

- Corrupt co-workers

- Stolen mail

Cases of identity theft are most often committed by someone you already know. Many cases go unnoticed. You can be unaware of any theft until you apply for a credit card or receive a notification from a collection agency.

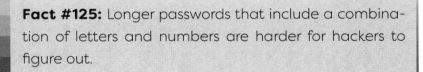

Fact #125: Longer passwords that include a combination of letters and numbers are harder for hackers to figure out.

If you suspect an account has been hacked, your first step to prevent further complications is to change your username and passwords to any online accounts. If you become aware of any charges to accounts that weren't authorized by you or any other account user, steps should be taken to close and reopen the account. This will help prevent any further illegal purchases. Credit card representatives are often just a phone call away to help you with these complicated procedures.

Fact #126: Account passwords should be creative, but also easy to remember.

Many financial institutions are encouraging customers to migrate to electronic methods of paying bills and monitoring accounts. These companies believe your financial information is safer being accessed through usernames, passwords, and PINs rather than using standard postal delivery. While it may be a safer and more convenient alternative to paper mail, electronic accounts can still be infiltrated.

Fact #127: By using complex passwords, signing credit cards immediately upon arrival, and shredding receipts, unused card offers, and personal financial documents, you help decrease the likelihood of fraud.

Be sure to take precautions in safeguarding your account. The proper steps can help protect you against the prying eyes of identity thieves.

Your credit report can be a great tool for finding incidences of identity theft. Sometimes the mistakes that show up on your credit report are the result of typographical errors. Other times, it means that someone has access to your personal information and has been using it to open accounts in your name. You are entitled to a free credit report from each of the three credit bureaus once per year. Review your credit score at least three times per year to check for accuracy. If anything looks peculiar or you know that it is inaccurate, report it immediately. The sooner you report it, the easier it is to fix.

—Amber Berry, certified financial education instructor and certified money coach

Gone Phishing?

Technology has made it easier for identity thieves to trick you into giving them valuable financial access. Phishing is a common method of identity theft. It involves a stranger pretending to be someone you know in an effort to obtain your personal information. These messages are often text-based and can appear in email or social media posts.

 Fact #128: Besides email and spyware, phishing scams can also occur through phone calls and social media posts.

Phishing can also be successful through the use of spyware. Spyware is a computer program that is downloaded without your knowledge. It scans your computer for valuable pieces of account information like passwords or access codes. Sometimes visiting infected websites can damage your hard-drive with menacing spyware programs.

 Fact #129: Email systems do not have the advanced security measures that appear on most websites. Avoid logging into accounts through email links.

Spyware programs do exactly what their name implies; they spy on computer systems. Most programs are fully automated. They snoop around your computer for specific files and transfer them back to a criminal over an Internet connection. Other programs perform keyboard captures. As you type in your username, password, or other sensitive information, the program makes a copy of your keyboard input.

 Fact #130: When a user is on a secure website, a padlock icon will appear on the browser page.

Most phishing scams are preventable. A combination of anti-virus software and good online security habits are often enough to prevent identity theft. Below are some of the steps you can take to protect your computer system and your online identity:

- Be suspicious of emails requesting personal information.

- Refuse to supply personal information over unsecured networks

- Be suspicious of emails that are not personalized

- Never click on links from unfamiliar contacts

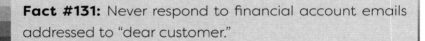

Fact #131: Never respond to financial account emails addressed to "dear customer."

Remember, a legitimate financial institution will never ask you to submit personal information through email. If you suspect you are the victim of a phishing scam, you can file a report with the Internet Crime Complaint Center (ICCC).

Many people deal with identity theft each year. Some of it comes from credit fraud. My bank accounts were hacked a few times a couple of years ago. When I spoke to my attorney about it, he informed me that people were obtaining illegal copies of people's credit reports on the black market. It's crucial that we keep our financial and personal information secure at all times. With advancements in technology, we are able to do more things online. Therefore, the internet is like a playground for these thieves.

—JeFreda Brown, MBA, business consultant and CEO of Goshen Business Group, LLC

Fraud Alerts

Even if you've never been a victim of identity theft, it might be a good idea to add fraud alerts to your various accounts. Placing fraud alerts in your credit files or accounts will help to cutoff potential criminal activity. These alerts can notify you almost immediately of illegal credit card purchases or withdrawals made to non-recognized accounts. If using a company's mobile application, a fraud alert can consist of something as simple as a pop-up notification.

Fact #132: Accessing your account from an unrecognized computer or from another geographic location can mistakenly trigger a fraud alert. These errors only demonstrate that your alert system is actively preventing identity thieves from accessing your information.

Fraud alerts are especially helpful to active duty military personnel. Soldiers heading overseas for a long deployment have more important concerns than the status of their credit file. These security measures provide consumers with an added sense of well-being knowing that their account history is under the watchful eyes of trusted financial institutions.

Fact #133: Activating fraud alerts is a helpful security measure if travelling overseas for an extended period of time.

One way to prevent identity theft is to place fraud alerts on your bank accounts, credit cards, and credit reports. This will cause you to receive immediate alerts or notifications when something fishy happens. It helps catch unauthorized transactions.

—JeFreda Brown, MBA, business consultant and CEO of Goshen Business Group, LLC

Security Freezes

Another method of protecting yourself from identity theft is a security freeze. It is a more complicated procedure than activating fraud alerts, but can act as a barrier against identity thieves attempting to access your accounts. A security freeze prevents credit reporting agencies from making new inquiries into your account. It will not affect accounts that are already established in your credit file.

Fact #134: While a security freeze is a great safety net, it is not 100 percent effective against identity theft. Many businesses can still issue credit without consulting your file.

If someone gained access to your personal information and attempted to apply for a line of credit, the security freeze would prevent that card company from making an inquiry. This roadblock would prevent that line of credit from being approved and the identity thief would be unable to open an account in your name.

A security freeze isn't for everyone. If you are looking to buy a home, car, or other major purchase, a security freeze would prevent even yourself from gaining new access to credit. If you are in a stage in your life where you aren't looking to open new credit accounts, then a freeze is a more appropriate strategy.

If you've initiated a freeze and need access to open a new credit account, you can apply for a temporary lift of your security freeze. These requests must be made in writing to the major reporting agencies. It may take a few days for the temporary lift to begin, so leave yourself plenty of time to make this adjustment to your credit file.

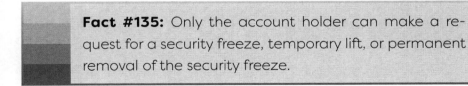

Fact #135: Only the account holder can make a request for a security freeze, temporary lift, or permanent removal of the security freeze.

To start an account freeze, you will need to supply your personal information along with proof of identity like a current utility bill. There are usually fees associated with initiating an account freeze and you'll be expected to pay them. Personal check, money order, or credit card are all acceptable forms of payment.

Some companies may request a copy of the report detailing any identity theft crimes before granting a security freeze. Making sure to have all of your paperwork in order will ease the security freeze application process.

 Fact #136: If your confirmation number is lost or forgotten, it will affect the processing of security freeze removal.

The credit reporting agency will send you a confirmation letter and number after your security freeze has begun. Keep this information in a safe place; you'll need it to temporarily or permanently remove the freeze.

 Fact #137: Unlike fraud alerts, a fee is required to activate, stop, or remove a security freeze from credit files.

In some situations, you won't have to pay for a security freeze. Most states will offer free security freezes if you are found to be a victim of identity theft.

 Fact #138: A security freeze request made to one major reporting agency must be honored by the others.

Identity Theft and Social Security Numbers

If your life has been completely flipped upside-down by identity theft, there is one final action you can take. The Social Security Administration (SSA) in the past has allowed the change of social security numbers in extreme cases. Individuals in the witness protection program or victims of extreme domestic abuse have been permitted to change their federal ID number.

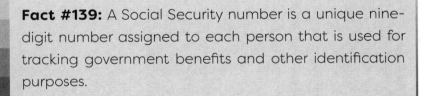

Fact #139: A Social Security number is a unique nine-digit number assigned to each person that is used for tracking government benefits and other identification purposes.

In the case of overwhelming financial attacks against your credit identity, the federal government may allow you to receive a new social security number. The process is long and complicated. There are many documents to file in order to successfully assume a new number. In recent years, there have been a variety of homeland security issues that have only made this process more difficult.

Fact #140: You can find more information about changing your Social Security number by contacting the SSA or visiting their website at www.socialsecurity.gov.

Your state's Department of Motor Vehicles (DMV) will also allow you to change your driver's license number if necessary. The amount of paperwork varies on a state-to-state basis, so it is best to check with your state's rules regarding such a change.

Fact #141: Changing your Social Security number is a highly complex process. Be prepared to oversee all record changes personally, because the government will not.

Identity Theft and Computers

It is important to understand the procedures for protecting your home PC or laptop from cyber criminals. By making some very simple changes, you can help reduce the risk of having your personal information stolen from your own hard drive.

If you receive an email or phone call from someone claiming to be your bank, insurance company, or any other organization, and they are asking you to verify your financial or personal information, do not. Never give your information over the phone to anyone who calls you first. This is one way many scammers get people's information. Never click on links in emails that look suspicious. This is how hackers plant viruses on your devices.

—JeFreda Brown, MBA, business consultant and CEO of Goshen Business Group, LLC

A few tips for protecting your computer are:

- Keep your laptop close to you when out in public

- Minimize or close files when away from the screen

- Use a password

- Don't keep a list of account passwords saved on your computer

- Install anti-virus software

- Delete unnecessary or unused personal information

Fact #142: Make sure to logout of your financial account websites after each session. This will help lower the risk of someone accessing your information.

Identity Theft and Smartphones

Smartphones are quickly becoming just as powerful as laptops and PCs. Many consumers are using the convenience of smartphone apps to make payments and check account balances with just the swipe of a finger. While these devices are easing access to your banking and credit card information, they are a rising source of ID theft.

You can help protect your smartphone by:

- Using a password or fingerprint ID

- Log out of financial apps after each session

- Don't use an unsecured Wi-Fi network

- Have a plan in place if you lose or misplace your phone

Fact #143: Be careful using an unsecured or public Wi-Fi network. You never know who could be lurking on it.

Identity Theft and the Mailbox

If you still prefer the feel of putting pen to paper, or enjoy licking and stuffing envelopes, then paying your bills by mail is the way to go. While it doesn't offer the same ease or timeliness of payment as online transactions, some consumers feel more trust regarding this method.

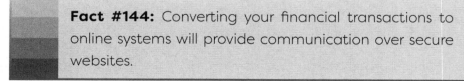

Fact #144: Converting your financial transactions to online systems will provide communication over secure websites.

Below are some helpful tips for safeguarding your financial correspondence:

- Use locked mailboxes or a P.O. box

- Mail payments and other sensitive information from the post office

- Request your bank hold new check orders until you can safely pick them up

> **Fact #145:** A P.O. Box, or post office box, is a locked mailbox held within a post office.

Under the Fair Credit Billing Act, you are only liable for unauthorized credit card charges up to $50. If there are any unauthorized charges in your credit card account due to identity theft, you are not liable for any of the charges. If you lose your card or someone steals it, you may be liable for up to $50 of unauthorized charges if you report the charges after your card is used.

—JeFreda Brown, MBA, business consultant and CEO of Goshen Business Group, LLC

CHAPTER 8

Bankruptcy—The Dreaded "B-Word"

I t's the word no one wants to talk about. Maybe you've heard your parents talking about it in hushed tones, or another family member has been directly affected by it. Whether you want to or not, bankruptcy should be a part of your financial vocabulary. Hopefully, this isn't an issue you need to be concerned about now, but as you grow older it's a topic on which you'll want to have some education.

Bankruptcy laws exist to help consumers invest in a business or take other financial risks. These laws can provide protection against creditors coming to collect if a business fails or an investment results in a major loss. There are many negative stereotypes associated with bankruptcy. You might conjure an image of a poor, penniless businessman sitting on a street corner hanging his head in shame.

The truth is bankruptcy affects us all. Without bankruptcy protection, the risks associated with borrowing money would be so high that consumers wouldn't take on the debt. Borrowing money is a major piece in the U.S. economic puzzle.

Fact #146: More than one million American families file for bankruptcy protection each year.

The concept of bankruptcy is fairly simple. If you are unable to pay back money owed despite your best efforts, you can file for bankruptcy protection. That doesn't mean you have to declare bankruptcy for all of your debts. You can request to keep some debt if you can prove to the bankruptcy court that you have the ability to pay it. This is called reaffirmation.

Reaffirmation is a good strategy for rebuilding credit scores. Make sure you are certain you can afford to pay the specified debt. You should check with creditors that the terms to your account don't change after a bankruptcy declaration. You don't want to encounter a higher interest rate on the back-end of your filing.

> Credit score is critical—but so are the elements comprising the credit score. People often make the mistake of thinking that credit score is all that matters with credit. What's more important is why your credit score is the number it is. For example, is your credit score a 700 because you are young and have a few accounts that you have been paying on time for a couple of years? Or, is your credit score 700 because you had an excellent credit history for 10 years, but you had a bankruptcy 3 years ago and are just rebuilding your credit? Is your credit score a 700 because you had a great history of paying 4 trade lines (car payment, one student loan, and, two credit cards) on time for 3 or more years, but you missed a medical bill and it was sent to collections?
>
> —Elysia Stobbe, mortgage expert and bestselling author

Bankruptcy protection is a legal way for individuals or businesses to start over. Without it, some consumers would never be able to recover and regain a normal life. Bankruptcy protection is established through the court system. By filing, a judge can put a stop to fees, penalties and threats made by creditors.

Many people file for bankruptcy protection each year. The reasons associated with the need to file vary from situation to situation. The bankruptcy code breaks down the types of bankruptcy into chapters.

Below is a list of bankruptcy chapters and their purpose:

- Chapter 7 - Liquidation

- Chapter 9 - Municipalities

- Chapter 11 - Companies

- Chapter 12 - Farmers

- Chapter 13 - Wage Earner

The two most common filing codes are Chapter 7 and 13. In a Chapter 7 filing, you are required to sell, or liquidate, some of your possessions to help pay for money you owe. In a Chapter 13 filing, you are allowed to keep your assets, but must make payments toward your debt that are arranged and supervised by the courts.

 Fact #147: More than half of all bankruptcy cases are the result of uninsured medical costs.

Not all debts are protected under bankruptcy laws. Some must be paid regardless of filing for bankruptcy protection.

Debts not protected from bankruptcy filings include:

- Taxes

- Alimony

- Child support

- Student loans

You will be expected to pay these debts in full no matter your current financial standing.

The BAPCPA

In 2005, Congress passed the Bankruptcy Abuse Prevention and Consumer Protection Act (BAPCPA). This set of laws places certain restrictions on bankruptcy filings and helps prevent consumers from abusing the right to declare bankruptcy.

Fact #148: The Bankruptcy Abuse Prevention and Consumer Protection Act specifies that no major credit card purchases can be made within 90 days of filing.

The BAPCPA requires you to attend credit counseling sessions from an approved, non-profit credit counseling agency before filing for bankruptcy. The act also enforces limits on spending and borrowing behavior.

Depending on which chapter you choose to file under, you will be expected to supply the courts with financial disclosures and other paperwork. You and your attorney will develop a budget and plan that the court will approve as an acceptable method of paying off your debts. The act also gives certain rights to creditors. They have the right to view a copy of your tax returns to confirm that you have the inability to pay back what you owe.

Fact #149: Under Chapter 13, consumers are required to submit tax information from the last four years.

During the time between when you file for bankruptcy and it is discharged from your credit report, you will be asked to complete a financial management course. This course will be taught by a credit counseling agency or other educational institution. The course must be approved by the court.

A final requirement of the BAPCPA is that consumers must wait a certain number of years after filing before filing a second time. No matter how bad your situation gets, you can't keep relying on this method of recovery.

Fact #150: The BAPCPA states a period of eight years for Chapter 7 and two years for Chapter 13 must pass before filing for bankruptcy a second time.

Bankruptcy Protection Tests

Chapter 7 bankruptcy is the most popular filing code in the United States. Because of the high number of consumers abusing bankruptcy protection, the government has placed certain conditions on filing requirements. The bankruptcy court will make a full investigation into your finances and make a decision on whether or not to allow you to file.

There are a series of tests designed to examine your account history and see if you have the ability to pay all or part of your debt. These three tests focus on your level of income and identify those eligible for bankruptcy protection under Chapter 7. You'll only need to meet the requirements of one of the three tests to qualify for protection.

The first test calculates if your income is below the median level set by your state. The bankruptcy court will request copies of your tax returns to help them reach a decision. Median income is based on the size of a household and varies from state to state.

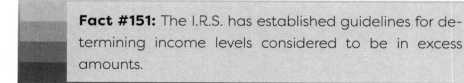

Fact #151: The I.R.S. has established guidelines for determining income levels considered to be in excess amounts.

The second test analyzes your excess monthly income. After looking at your budget, if the bankruptcy court deems your excess income is over a specified amount, you will not be granted bankruptcy protection.

The final test focuses once again on excess income. If your income is above a specified amount for more than five years, and you'll be able to pay off more than 25 percent of debts owed, the court will forbid you from filing.

If you encounter challenges passing any of these three tests, you may still qualify for protection under Chapter 13. This chapter has similar filing requirements and is often the next filing strategy for consumers facing the inability to settle debts.

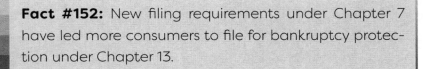

Fact #152: New filing requirements under Chapter 7 have led more consumers to file for bankruptcy protection under Chapter 13.

Chapter 13 filing requirements are much like Chapter 7. They both require credit counseling and the submission of tax returns as proof of income. After the court calculates income levels, a decision to allow filing privileges is granted. The main differences between the two filing chapters relates to the time periods allowing repayment.

A Big Decision

Hopefully, you'll never have to deal with the stresses associated with filing for bankruptcy. The decision to declare bankruptcy will have an impact on your life for years to come. This decision will affect your bank accounts, credit reports, and your self-image. Bankruptcy filings can remain on your credit report for up to ten years, so be sure to evaluate all of your options before making this difficult call.

Fact #153: Bankruptcy may only act as a temporary "band-aid" in some situations. An examination of your spending habits will help identify the true causes of your growing debt.

In today's society, bankruptcy filings reflect a negative financial characteristic. Some people view individuals who file for bankruptcy as "bad people". Regardless of popular opinion, filing may be the only way out of your monetary troubles. No matter what you or others think about bankruptcy, if you have no realistic way to pay back money you borrowed, this is one last chance to move forward in your financial life.

Before making the decision to file, you should consider the following:

- Make sure a bankruptcy filing will SOLVE your financial problems

- Examine how a filing will affect your future goals

- Consider long-term consequences

- Explore other ways of reducing debt

- Get professional opinions on whether or not to file

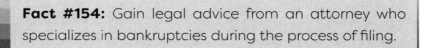

Fact #154: Gain legal advice from an attorney who specializes in bankruptcies during the process of filing.

When bills keep piling up and collection agencies won't stop calling or filling your inbox, you'll be tempted to jump right into the filing process. It is important to take the time you need and seek assistance in moving forward with a bankruptcy declaration.

Fact #155: Before filing, contact your creditors directly to discuss possible repayment plans that could still be an option in settling debts.

Wait . . .

Even after filing your bankruptcy paperwork, you can still change your mind. But that doesn't mean that everything goes back to the way it was before. There are still consequences associated with flip-flopping on your decision to claim bankruptcy protection.

You can request to have the court dismiss your case as long as the request is made before the bankruptcy is discharged from your credit report. Your credit file will still show the bankruptcy filing and your credit score will be affected for many years after. However, credit reporting agencies will be required to list that the bankruptcy case was dismissed.

Fact #156: After filing, the decision not to pursue bankruptcy protection can have lasting effects.

. . . No, go ahead.

Changing your mind is one thing, but repeatedly wavering back and forth can drive someone crazy. Imagine going to the movies with friends. At first, you want to see the big-budget superhero blockbuster. While in line, you decide instead to see the latest zombie apocalypse thriller. Finally, at the ticket window you settle back to the superhero movie. This back-and-forth would drive your friends bonkers!

Bankruptcy laws include rules for similar flip-flopping. Filing, requesting a dismissal, and then re-filing again is only permitted if all three occur in less than one year. There are consequences associated with this failure to make a decision. Collection activity will be suspended, but only for a limited amount of time. You will also be limited in the number of times you are allowed to declare bankruptcy.

Fact #157: Flip-flopping on your filing decision requires you to complete all required paperwork and credit counseling within 30 days or collection activities will resume.

Life After Bankruptcy

Bankruptcy is not a reset button. It isn't like a video game where you can just start over again. It may stop debt collectors, numerous added payments and fees, and threats of legal action, but there will still be other consequences. After the dust settles, you will be faced with the challenges of rebuilding your financial life. Be prepared to rebuild your credit profile, use credit more carefully going forward, and be ready to explain your bankruptcy filing when you apply for future credit.

Obtaining credit

Despite a bankruptcy appearing in your credit file, some credit card companies will still consider your application. The companies understand that you won't be able to declare bankruptcy again for many years. They know you'll agree to accept higher interest rates on accounts because of your shaky financial history.

Fact #158: Account histories included in the bankruptcy will be shortened. This can negatively affect your credit score.

Because of your history of bankruptcy, you are already at a disadvantage moving forward. Some lenders will try to take advantage of your situation by signing you to contracts that contain added fees, penalties, and higher-than-normal interest rates.

Be sure to seek out a responsible post-bankruptcy credit lender. You don't want to experience any added stress or financial difficulty due to an abusive credit relationship.

Fact #159: Only secured debts, like mortgages, will remain open after a bankruptcy. Unsecured debts, such as credit cards, will be closed.

The status of your credit score before a bankruptcy is very important. The better your score before a filing is made, the more your score will drop. If you already had a bad credit score to begin with, your score won't be lowered that much. The same parts of a credit file that determine your credit score are also influenced by a bankruptcy.

After you file for bankruptcy, you will be contacted by companies claiming to be able to help. Your name and information will be added to mailing lists for various financial recovery companies. These companies will make you offers on packages they say can help you start a new life after bankruptcy. If it gets to be too much, you can opt-out of these mailings by contacting the appropriate marketing association.

Fact #160: New credit applications will be needed after a bankruptcy to help reignite your credit history.

Be prepared to compose a written statement. This statement can be placed in your credit file to help explain the details surrounding your bankruptcy. Keep it positive and upbeat. It is best if you can connect your bankruptcy to a single event like a divorce or illness. If poor financial habits are to blame for your situation, try to show that you have grown from the experience and learned better ways to manage your credit habits.

Renting

Finding an apartment after a bankruptcy can present its own set of challenges. Landlords and property management companies can obtain copies of your credit report before entering into a rental agreement. A bankruptcy might not mean you will be denied a lease on a property, but you can expect an increase in a security deposit or the need to have a cosigner on the contract.

Insurance

In some states, insurance companies can factor in credit scores in their decision to grant coverage to consumers. After examining your credit report, a bankruptcy filing could raise your insurance premium rates. Home and auto insurance companies are more likely to view credit reports than medical insurers.

Fact #161: A bankruptcy can prevent an employer from issuing certain security clearances or licenses.

Employment

It is illegal for a company to deny you employment because of a bankruptcy. After viewing your credit history, a company may refuse to hire you but will give another reason and not even mention the bankruptcy.

Self Image

Many people draw a connection between their financial wealth and self-worth. Financial collapse, like a bankruptcy, can have a negative effect on your mental and emotional state. Post-bankruptcy lifestyle changes can be so drastic, they can drive people to depression. It is important to seek counseling and other therapy services should a bankruptcy start to affect your personal life.

Obtaining a mortgage

Fact #162: After filing for a Chapter 13 bankruptcy, you can apply for a mortgage after completing one year of payments under a certified repayment plan.

Getting approval for a mortgage is not an easy process for anyone. Even with a strong credit history, there are many qualifications necessary for the successful approval of a loan. A bankruptcy filing in your past doesn't immediately disqualify you from getting a mortgage; however, it will make the process an uphill battle.

If you can convince a mortgage lender that the financial issues associated with your bankruptcy are firmly in your past, you will have a better chance of getting your loan application approved. If your bankruptcy has cleared your credit file and you've re-established a positive credit history in your name, you'll have even better chances.

The type of loan you are offered by a lender can vary. After a bankruptcy, a mortgage company is more likely to offer you a bargain-basement loan. These lower-quality loans are more likely to be approved if your credit history is poor due to a bankruptcy. These loans usually cost more. They carry higher interest rates, fees, and need more than a standard down payment to begin the agreement.

Fact #163: Mortgage investors divide loans into A, B, C, or D categories based on the overall quality of the loan.

Debt Management vs. Bankruptcy

A benefit of receiving credit counseling during a time of financial difficulty is establishing a debt management plan. Most credit card companies will accept the terms of a debt management plan because it guarantees they will still receive some payments. In the instance of a bankruptcy, the companies will receive no payments at all.

Fact #164: A debt management plan has less restrictions than a Chapter 13 bankruptcy filing.

A debt management plan offers many advantages over bankruptcy. It is less intrusive to your spending habits and is less likely to damage your credit score. Even after filing, you can still declare bankruptcy if the debt management plan fails to help your financial situation.

Payments

Debt management plans allow payments to be made to creditors in addition to any interest rate increases or other fees. Debt management plans can also benefit you by lowering these higher-interest charges or fees. In some cases, a creditor cannot profit from the debt management agreement at all. Under Chapter 7, a creditor cannot apply any additional interest charges. Chapter 13 has a similar protection measure.

Fact #165: Under Chapter 13 protection, a creditor will lose the difference between the current debt balance and the cost of the original debt.

Disposable income

Disposable income is money left over after paying living expenses and any debts owed. Under a debt management plan, any money left over after monthly payments and other itemized expenses (such as groceries and utility bills) are put into a separate account. Chapter 13 bankruptcy requires that all leftover disposable income be paid back to creditors to help settle owed payments.

Fact #166: Many credit card companies do not report debt management plans to credit reporting agencies. Those that do will list it in the description of included accounts.

CHAPTER 9

Maintaining Good Credit

During your education, parents and teachers have taught you the skills necessary to maintain a good GPA. Good study skills, turning in assignments on time, and always being prepared with your classroom supplies are just a few of the tools necessary to keep your grades up. Your credit score is no different. Taking the time to make sure your finances are in order and following the best budgeting strategies can help you keep your rating in the upper region of credit scores.

A good credit rating can help improve your relationship with card companies and grant you lower interest rates on major purchases. You should always be up to date on the status of your credit score. Salespeople may try to take advantage of your lack of credit score knowledge. They may lead you to believe you are a credit risk, when you are not. By keeping a watchful eye on your credit thermometer, you'll be able to take swift action if your score dips into those colder temperatures.

Making regular credit score check-ups is not the only way to maintain good credit health. Reducing debt, holding different credit types, paying bills on time, and carrying a lower credit balance are all useful strategies in keeping a strong credit score.

Maintaining good credit can be easy! Pay what you owe when it's due, don't borrow more than you can afford to pay back, and you will be fine. What often causes trouble for people is not taking action when things go awry. If you encounter challenging life circumstances, be proactive and contact your lenders instead of avoiding them. It's not a pleasant call to make, but it can also be unpleasant to for file bankruptcy unnecessarily. Should you ever find yourself in trouble, reach out for advice and help from a trusted professional.

—Amber Berry, certified financial education instructor and certified money coach

Fact #167: Credit reports should be inspected at least three months before making a major purchase.

A Healthy Balance

Good eating habits are the landmark of a healthy diet. You want to make sure your daily intake of fruits and vegetables is in balance with your intake of dairy and grains. A healthy ratio of differing types of credit is also essential to your credit health. To improve your credit score you'll want a mix of credit cards, retail accounts, mortgages, finance accounts, and installment loans. This list of mixed credit sources sends a positive message to lenders. It shows that you are capable of handling varying types of repayment responsibilities.

Be careful to not take on too many accounts. A selection of mixed credit accounts is not a requirement in determining a good credit score, but if you do take on multiple accounts, there should be a nice mix of payment schedules. At least one of your accounts should be an installment loan. These loans will help your credit score the most.

Fact #168: New credit accounts should be acquired over time and not all at once.

Installment loans

Fact #169: Stores that display ads reading "no interest" or "no payment" for a set period of time are advertising installment loans.

This type of loan is common among stores that sell products in higher price ranges. It is often seen in furniture and appliance stores. The price tag on a sofa or new washer/dryer is often more than the average consumer can afford in one payment. These stores offer financing over a period of time and at a set interest rate. If you've seen commercials where the spokesperson shouts "NO INTEREST FOR 6 MONTHS", they are pitching an installment loan.

Non-installment loans

Non-installment loans are accounts where the balance must be paid in full at the end of each month. These types of accounts are not very popular because of the inability to carry a balance from one month to the next. The advantage of non-installment loans is it helps you be more responsible with your spending and keeps your debt from adding up too quickly.

> There are multiple steps in creating a good financial plan. The first thing you need to do is look at your current finances. You can do this by creating a budget. You can also create an income statement and balance sheet for your personal finances. Using the debt-to-income ratio and the debt safety ratio will also help. Next, develop your financial goals. You should look at short term and long term goals. After that, you are ready to develop your action plan and implement it. Finally, consistently check your progress and make revisions where needed.
>
> —JeFreda Brown, MBA, business consultant and CEO of Goshen Business Group, LLC

Revolving loans

The best example of a revolving loan is the traditional credit card. With this type of loan you have the option of paying the bill in full each month, or carrying a balance forward with you to the next month. You will be required to make at least the minimum payment each month. This minimum amount is designated by the credit card company and is based on your account balance.

Credit cards

Throughout your financial life, you will have an almost daily interaction with credit cards. To ease payment timeliness, many monthly bills can be sent directly to a specific credit card account. Smartphones can even hold your account information in a "virtual" credit card. No longer do you have to swipe your card at a checkout. Like a magic wand, modern technology allows you to pay for purchases with a simple wave of your phone.

Fact #170: After the Fair Credit and Charge Card Disclosure Act passed in 1989, credit card companies were forced to provide interest rates and fees to consumers before they accepted an offer on a line of credit.

So, which card should you choose? With so many offers piling up, let's take a look at some of your options.

Visa and Mastercard

The two most popular credit cards available are Visa and Mastercard. It is important to understand that Visa and Mastercard DO NOT issue lines of credit. They are simply a card services provider. Banks or other lending institutions can use their services to issue credit cards. Visa and Mastercard set forth basic rules about card usage and processing, but all fees and interest rates are established by the banks doing the lending. If you are rejected for a Visa card by one lender, that doesn't mean you will be rejected for all future Visa card applications.

It is common for consumers to hold more than one of each of these cards. They are accepted by almost every store and business around the world. Be sure to keep one in your wallet.

> It takes discipline when dealing with credit. You have to use strong self-control. It's good to just start out with one credit card. Try to only use it when you have an emergency and when you know you will be able to pay the balance off. Try to keep the balance low on the card. The rule of thumb is to keep the balance below 30 percent of the available credit limit.
>
> —JeFreda Brown, MBA, business consultant and CEO of Goshen Business Group, LLC

Discover card

A major competitor to Visa and Mastercard and another horse in your credit card stable is the Discover card. This card, made available by Discover Financial Services, started as a direct competitor to Visa and Mastercard. Its major draw to consumers was its one percent cash back rebate on purchases. This card paid you to use it. It was a big hit among cardholders. If you don't travel much, it is a great addition to your wallet. The Discover card is only accepted at U.S. businesses.

Fact #171: Discover cards are available in a Classic, Gold, and Platinum edition. Each level offers its own unique set of benefits.

American Express

The American Express card is often viewed as the crown jewel of credit cards. Their advertisements feature celebrities and they target an audience interested in luxury and status. This card is best known for its lack of a credit limit. American Express allows approved customers to make purchases freely. Their customer service representatives only take action if they feel a customer is making purchases beyond what they consider to be appropriate.

Fact #172: American Express uses software to track their customer's spending habits.

Home equity loans

If you own a home, you can use it to your advantage. A home equity loan allows you to borrow money against the value of your home. The bank assigns a value to your home, and offers you a loan based on that value. If you are financially disciplined, and you don't see any reasons why your home value might drop, then a home equity loan may be a good option for you.

Fact #173: A home equity line of credit can be obtained for 50 to 80 percent of a home's total value.

If you become unable to make payments to the bank who supplies the loan, they can take your house. Home equity loans are also known for variable interest rates. These rates can change over time and respond to current economic forecasts. In the past, some subprime lenders were offering home equity loans for amounts over 100 percent of the home's total value. This risky lending practice was a factor in the 2007 collapse of the housing market. The home equity loan can be a risky option. Take the proper steps to safeguard your borrowing.

> **Fact #174:** The interest rate on a home equity loan is often lower than other types of loans. However, that doesn't mean there aren't other hidden risks.

Personal loans

Personal loans are offered by most banks. Banks are more likely to offer these loans to existing customers. You should inquire about loan options with any customer service representative at your local branch. They can assist you with questions on interest rates or any other fees. A personal loan is a great tool for consolidating debt.

> **Fact #175:** If you already have a card with a high credit limit and low interest rate, a personal loan may not be a necessary option for you.

Joint credit

Managing your own credit can be a challenge. If you have a joint credit account, you also have to be concerned with your partner's credit habits. Joint accounts are the responsibility of both people. Financial documents related to the joint credit account will appear in the credit files of each consumer.

> **Fact #176:** In a joint credit account, both parties sign a contract agreeing to make adequate and timely payments.

Managing Credit Accounts

Proper credit account management involves good organizational skills and attention to detail. A close inspection of the terms of a credit agreement is of the greatest importance. Contracts that involve making payments over a period of months or years are not so easy to get out of. Even if you decide to cancel the contract, you may still be expected to pay what is owed. This is common in cell phone contracts where the cost of the phone is built into the monthly payment. You can't keep your shiny new device until the balance is paid off. There is no such thing as a free phone.

> Sometimes things happen that are unavoidable or not your fault, and they can cause you fall behind on debt payments. In order to maintain good credit, making timely payments is critical. If you run into trouble financially, contact your creditors to discuss programs they may offer to help you get back on track.
>
> —JeFreda Brown, MBA, business consultant and CEO of Goshen Business Group, LLC

Paying down your debt is still the best way to manage your credit accounts. It can reduce your interest rates and increase your credit score. Keep track of your account credit limits and calculate the amount of debt spread out over those accounts. If you find you are using more than 50 percent of your available credit limit, stop spending and start funneling money towards those bills.

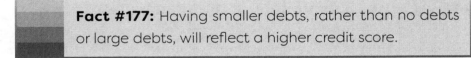

Fact #177: Having smaller debts, rather than no debts or large debts, will reflect a higher credit score.

Choosing a credit card

The cost of a credit card is not easily calculated. It can get really confusing with all the offers bombarding you on a daily basis. Interest rates, annual fees, and other costs are always changing. Fairly priced card offers are out there, but they are more difficult to come by. You'll have to do your homework, but finding the right card is worth your time.

Fact #178: A credit card disclosure table should be included on all credit offers you receive. It lists interest rates and other fees associated with the account.

When considering which card to choose, you'll want to look at four key areas: interest rates, annual fees, grace periods, and additional fees. These credit card characteristics should be your focus when researching possible card candidates.

Interest rates

Interest rates are the primary method in which credit card companies make a profit. These finance charges are additional fees, bundled into your monthly payment, that you must pay for the ability to borrow money. For most cards, if the balance is not paid in full at the end of each month, an interest fee is charged. Each credit card will list an Annual Percentage Rate (APR). This number indicates the amount of interest that will be charged over a one year period.

Annual fees

Some credit card companies require an annual fee to be paid just to use the card. This fee can range anywhere from $0 to $100, with the average being $20. If a company doesn't charge an annual fee, they rely on interest charges as a way to make money. If a card carries an annual fee AND and high interest rate, you'd benefit from continuing your credit search.

Grace periods

If you choose to mail a check rather than use electronic payments, then grace periods can be an advantage for you. Grace periods are the timeframe from when a payment is due and when a billing cycle ends. As long as full payment arrives before a specific cut-off date, no additional interest or late fees will be charged. It can assist customers who have a habit of making late or partial payments. If a credit card doesn't offer a grace period, interest will be applied regardless of whether the account is paid in full or not.

 Fact #179: Grace periods are only helpful to card holders who pay their balance in full each month.

Other fees

 Fact #180: Excessive late fees may result in an increase in interest rates on your credit card accounts.

The most common type of additional fees associated with credit cards are penalty fees. These fees are charged only if you violate a certain term of your card agreement with the company. These fees can be quite costly and add up quickly if you make a habit of breaking your credit contract. Penalty charges can include late payments, inactivity fees, exceeding your credit limit, or paying your monthly bill with a check that doesn't clear. Card companies use these fees as a way to increase profits. After you are hit with a penalty fee, the card company will charge interest on both your account balance and your penalties. Some companies even charge a fee for inactivity, or will close your account if it's inactive for a long period of time. Always do some research before opening a credit card account so you can avoid unnecessary fees.

Fact #181: Over-the-limit fees can range anywhere from $10 to $35 per month for balances in violation of account terms.

Types of credit users

Your financial personality plays a big role in your credit card usage. Do you have a budget? Do you stick to it? How do you pay for major purchases? Do you charge it, or save up the cash? These questions help figure out which credit user category you fall into.

There are three types of credit users, they are:

1. True credit users

2. Convenience users

3. Combination users

A true credit user is always active. They carry a balance from month to month and usually only pay the minimum balance. True credit users aren't concerned with annual fees or grace periods. Their focus is strictly on interest rates. If you find yourself in this category of credit user, be sure to seek out a card with the lowest rate available. Since you will be carrying a balance, you want to limit the amount of extra money you are paying to the card company.

A convenience user makes use of their credit card because it is easier, not because they don't have the cash. This credit card user likes to hurry through the checkout line and not stand around counting out their cash. Convenience users pay their account balance in full at the end of each month. Fitting this credit profile means you aren't concerned with interest rates like true credit users, because you always make timely payments for the full amount.

Combination users are a mix of both. Some months they pay the minimum, some months they pay it all. This type of credit user goes with the flow of life. If money is tight, they will carry a balance. During better times, they will make a payment to settle any debts owed. If this description sounds familiar, you might be a combo user.

 Fact #182: Combination users carry a balance about half the time and pay the balance in full the other half.

Reflect on your own credit habits to find which credit tribe you can call home.

How to save on credit card use

In the last section, you learned just how quickly interest rates and fees can add up. Credit cards can end up costing you more than you are willing to spend. There are two ways you can save money on your credit card accounts. The first is to contact customer service directly and request a lower interest rate. The second is to seek out a new card altogether and transfer your balance to the new card.

 Fact #183: Conversations with card companies may not yield a better interest rate offer if there is a negative credit history.

It never hurts to ask. The worst thing that can happen is your credit card company says no. If you are in good standing with your current card company, a request to waive fees or lower your interest rate may be met with approval. Card companies are not in the business of losing customers. If conversations with your card company don't result in you receiving a lower rate, you might want to consider switching to another card.

Credit card companies are in direct competition with each other. Making competitive offers is one way these companies can attract new consumers. One method for signing new customers is to offer balance transfers. A balance transfer is when a card company agrees to pay off your existing card debt by transferring your balance to one of their accounts in exchange for a fee. The fee is either a percentage of the amount transferred or a specific dollar amount, whichever is greater.

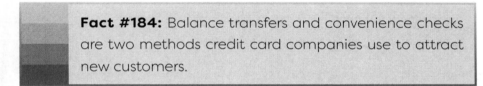

Fact #184: Balance transfers and convenience checks are two methods credit card companies use to attract new customers.

Hidden costs

Life can get pretty busy at times, and paying attention to your credit card bill can quickly take a backseat to other activities. It is important, however, to take a few minutes each month to look at the details of your credit agreement.

Hidden costs are not easy to find. If they were, they wouldn't be hidden! One way card companies gain a slight advantage is by charging interest from the date purchased and not the date posted. This minor detail can affect the length of time you are subject to interest charges. Just because you made a purchase on Friday night doesn't mean it will be posted to your account as soon as you hit "approve". Sometimes credit card charges can be pending for days before finally appearing on your statement.

Fact #185: Some card companies have minimum payments as low as 2 percent of the account balance.

Minimum payments is another strategy a card company can use against you. When a card company offers you a low minimum monthly payment, you may be pumping your fists in victory. Keep in mind that the less you pay each month, the longer it will take to pay off your debt and the more money you'll spend on interest.

A final advertising tactic companies employ is using 0 percent interest offers. These offers are great for balance transfers or to finance a major purchase. The problems arise when that promotional period ends. A high interest rate could kick in when you least expect it, leaving you with larger payments for any debt you've already taken on.

Fact #186: Many state laws allow card companies to change interest rates without reason, as long as advanced notice is given to the consumer.

Managing Insurance

There is no magic credit card that pays for trips to the emergency room. There is no zero percent interest gold card that will rebuild your house after a fire. For these disasters, you'll need insurance coverage. Most people overlook insurance as a part of maintaining good credit. Insurance is a necessity. It helps protect you and your assets should an unexpected situation arise. Understanding how insurance coverage affects your credit rating is a great first step in maintaining a positive credit reputation.

Life

After starting a family, you'll want to consider getting some degree of life insurance. Should you pass away, a life insurance company will make a payment to your family to help cover expenses in your absence. The most basic form of a life insurance policy is term life insurance. You make monthly payments over a specific period of time. At the end of the policy agreement, you can renew the term or take out a new policy for a higher or lower amount. The amount of the policy you choose will affect your monthly payment.

 Fact #187: A good life insurance policy should cover more than just funeral expenses.

Disability

Not having the ability to work can lead to many financial problems. If you experience an accident or illness that prevents you from performing your job, you'll wish you had some form of disability insurance. Disability insurance is designed to protect your income should you ever encounter an injury or illness that prevents you from working.

Home

The costs associated with home ownership are huge. Buying a house will probably be one of the biggest investments of your lifetime. Because of the financial commitments involved, you'll want to protect it. To help protect your home from fires, floods, and other natural disasters, you'll purchase some form of homeowner's insurance. This policy protects you if the need arises to make repairs or rebuild your home after a catastrophe. Most mortgages require some form of insurance before the loan will be approved. Be sure to shop around for a policy with excellent coverage. Homeowner's insurance policies can be included in your monthly mortgage payment so you won't have to worry about budgeting for an additional expense.

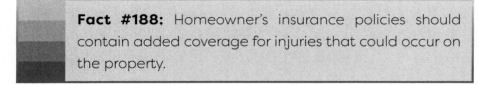

Fact #188: Homeowner's insurance policies should contain added coverage for injuries that could occur on the property.

Auto

After you pass your driver's test, you'll be thinking about buying a car. You should also get car insurance on your radar. Auto insurance protects both you and other drivers. In the event of an accident, if a claim is filed properly, your auto insurance company will help make payments for repairs.

Car insurance rates can change. Too many speeding tickets or fender bend-ers will surely cause your monthly payment to rise.

Fact #189: Most states require some form of car insur-ance in order to legally operate a motor vehicle.

What Doesn't Help?

You always want to put your best foot forward. In this final chapter, you learned about methods and strategies for maintaining a good credit history. Another helpful tool in your future economic travels is knowledge of what won't help your credit score.

There are many aspects of your financial life that can hurt your score and put you at a disadvantage in your efforts to obtain credit. There are also many tactics that won't make a difference to your score at all. This final section focuses on what won't help you on your journey. Let's take a look at these setbacks, roadblocks, and credit-helping mirages.

Closing old accounts

The length of your credit history plays a major role in calculating your credit score and the types of offers you receive. By closing old accounts, you are shortening this history and lowering your mix of account types. Even if a credit card is sitting in your wallet gathering dust, it might be a good idea to just let it sit if you have concerns about your credit history length, or if your limit is high and closing your account would affect your debt-to-credit ratio.

Fact #190: Closing negative accounts will not delete them from your credit report.

Late payments

A late payment is better than no payment, but it will still appear in your credit file. Whether it is late by five minutes or five days, late is late. Try to make timely payments to creditors. You can easily set smartphone reminders to alert you to upcoming due dates. Be sure to allow plenty of time if using the postal service to deliver your bills.

After obtaining credit, the main key to building your credit score is to make timely payments. Do this consistently. Missing a payment causes the creditor to report it as late. Once a late payment status appears on your credit report, it can lower your credit score. Also, missing one payment means you now have to make two payments or a double payment to get your account out of the late status.

—JeFreda Brown, MBA, business consultant and
CEO of Goshen Business Group, LLC

Fact #191: Attempts to make larger payments to make up for missed ones will not improve your credit score.

Negative credit filings

A negative filing is another way to hurt your credit standing. These scars on your credit file will only raise questions about their origins. Credit card companies will use these filings as the basis for denying your application. Don't give them a reason to reject you.

Fact #192: Lawsuits, legal judgments, and tax liens are all examples of negative credit filings.

Cosigning

Be careful who you vouch for or partner with in terms of credit accounts. Acting as a cosigner on a loan is a risky move if you are worried about your partner's financial future. If any negative entries are entered in their credit report, a copy will damage yours as well.

Fact #193: Until cosigned loan debts are settled, they will remain in the cosigner's credit file.

Other types of loans

Earlier in the book, you learned about finance company loans and the high level of risk associated with these low-quality lines of credit. Finance company loans are made to consumers with a poor credit background or those recovering from bankruptcy. These loans carry some of the highest interest rates in the industry. Even if you maintain a strong payment history with a loan from a finance company, credit reporting agencies may still view any activity on these loans as unfavorable.

Fact #194: Finance company loans can carry interest rates as high as 25 percent.

One of the riskiest and easiest ways to damage your good credit rating is to engage in the use of payday loans. These loans are structured through check-cashing businesses. Check cashing-businesses emerged as a way for consumers without bank accounts to cash in their paychecks. These businesses would profit by charging a fee on every check processed.

Payday loans help check-cashing businesses turn an even bigger profit. These loans are offered to customers with bad or no credit, or anyone who's desperately in need of money. If you fall into those categories, you might be vulnerable enough to take out a loan against your next check with little consideration for the additional cost. The interest rates on payday loans are huge and the requirements to open an account are minimal.

Fact #195: Many check-cashing businesses are not regulated and do not follow interest rate guidelines set by state laws.

Bankruptcy

Bankruptcy is the ultimate weapon against maintaining a good credit score. Many companies consider it the most negative entry one can have in their credit file. Even if you don't proceed after filing, the paper trail will still lead back to your credit file. This will impact your ability to take out loans and other forms of credit.

 Fact #196: The more recent your bankruptcy filing, the more likely your loan applications will be rejected.

Higher income

Even millionaires can have credit problems. Another myth in maintaining a good credit score is the higher your salary, the better your credit rating. Regardless of your income, a negative or short credit history will still have an impact on your credit score.

 Fact #197: Many credit card companies have a minimum income level established for accounts to be approved.

A higher income will only help you if you have a strong credit history, or it may help you obtain a higher credit limit when applying for a card. If you get a raise, be sure to contact your card services representative to inquire about making changes to your account agreement. You may be eligible for a higher credit limit, a lower interest rate, or other promotional offer.

 Fact #198: If you are self-employed, a card company may require you to submit copies of your tax returns as proof of income.

Pawnshops

Just like payday loans from check-cashing businesses, agreements with pawnshops should also be avoided. A pawnshop will accept your goods in return for a short-term cash loan. The agreements are very loosely structured and you can lose your belongings if you fail to honor the contract. The pawnshop can sell your items for a profit if you can't pay back your loan. It goes without saying that these loans have no benefit for your credit history and can only cause you aggravation and unneeded stress.

Fact #199: Loans from pawnshops usually only amount to a fraction of the cash value of the item you are leaving in the hands of the pawnbroker.

Conclusion

Congratulations! You made it! Your head is probably spinning with all the statistics and facts you've absorbed over the last nine chapters. No matter what decisions you make after graduation, keep in mind everything you've read in this book. This book should act as a reminder each time you open your wallet to make a purchase. Cash or credit? Spend or save? These are the questions you should ask before making both major and minor purchases.

Never underestimate the importance of your credit file. Make inquiries regularly for any inaccurate or fraudulent information. The contents can mean the difference between approval and rejection when applying for a credit card or mortgage. Take the steps necessary to protect yourself from identity theft (delve into the details and check out *The Young Adult's Guide to Identity Theft: A Step-by-Step Guide to Stopping Scammers*). If your negative credit situation is overwhelming you, seek help from a certified credit counselor. These are just a few of the helpful strategies you learned to help improve your credit score.

After 199 facts, you probably don't want to hear another one, but here it is . . . you're young. This puts you at a great advantage compared to millions of other consumers in the United States. You have the time to start making smart decisions *now*. Get a head start on preparing for college, a car, a home, and a future with endless possibility.

Credit card legislation and regulation is always changing. Do your homework. Research as much as you can about proposed changes to the laws surrounding credit scores. The road to financial success is long and winding. Luckily, you have some knowledge to guide your way.

Guest Contributors

Amber Berry is a millennial who shares her passion for personal finance through her website, **www.feelgoodfinances.com**. As a certified financial education instructor, certified money coach, and writer, she enjoys working with women and young adults to help them transform their relationships with money through education and compassion. She enjoys contributing to various online media outlets and staying caught up with the latest personal finance publications.

Mortgage expert and bestselling book author Elysia Stobbe has closed more than $250 million in residential mortgage loans during her career. As one of the nation's leading mortgage experts with more than 12 years of experience, Elysia has been featured in the Wall Street Journal, the Wall Street Business Radio Network, NPR and on FOX, ABC, NBC, CBS, and more for her expertise with VA mortgages and first time home buyers. Elysia has also been interviewed in U.S. News & World Report and Realtor.Com. Elysia is the author of the #1 best seller "How to Get Approved for the Best Mortgage Without Sticking a Fork in Your Eye," available online at ElysiaStobbeBooks.com.

As CEO of Goshen Business Group, LLC, JeFreda Brown provides financial and business compliance consulting for small to large sized businesses. With over 16 years of business experience, JeFreda is one of America's premier financial and business compliance consultants and subject matter experts. JeFreda earned her BS degree in math from Mississippi State University. She also has an MBA with a finance concentration from Mississippi College and an accounting concentration. She's the Author of *12 Reasons You Need an Accountant for Your Small Business*. JeFreda is also an adjunct finance professor, and she specializes in financial and business writing and copywriting.

Bibliography

Detweiler, Gerri. *The Ultimate Credit Handbook: Cut Your Debt and Have a Lifetime of Great Credit*. New York, NY: Plume, 2003. Print.

DiMaggio, Richard L. *Credit Repair: What the Credit Industry Doesn't Want You to Know*. Glenville, NY: Consumer, 2004. Print.

Fontinelle, Amy. "Best Ways to Get Free Credit Scores in 2016." *Investopedia*. N.p., 29 Apr. 2016. Web. 01 Feb. 2017.

"Frequently Asked Questions." *Internet Crime Complaint Center (IC3) | Home*. Federal Bureau of Investigation. Web. 14 Jan. 2017.

Hess, Donn. "Finding the Links Between Retirement, Stress, and Health." *Lockton Retirement Services* (2016): 1-6. 27 Apr. 2016. Web. 1 Feb. 2017.

"How It Works." *Credit Karma - Free Credit Reports*. Credit Karma. Web. 8 Jan. 2017.

"Learn about Scores." *MyFICO*. Web. 23 Dec. 2016.

Levin, Adam, and Beau Friedlander. *Swiped: How to Protect Yourself in a World Full of Scammers, Phishers, and Identity Thieves*. New York: Public Affairs, 2015. Print.

"Research, Statistics, & Policy Analysis." *The United States Social Security Administration*. U.S. Government. Web. 29 Dec. 2016.

Sember, Brette McWhorter. *The Complete Credit Repair Kit*. Naperville, IL: Sphinx Pub., 2011. Print.

Weston, Liz. *Your Credit Score: How to Improve the 3-Digit Number That Shapes Your Financial Future, Fourth Edition*. 5th ed.: FT, 2011. Print.

White, Michelle J. "Bankruptcy and Small Business." *Regulation: The CATO Review of Business and Government* 24.2 (2001): 18-20. Print.

Glossary

Adverse action letter – If your credit card application is reviewed and rejected, you will receive an adverse action letter detailing specific reasons as to why your application was rejected, and what reporting agency they obtained your credit report from.

Algorithm – A complex mathematical formula used in the calculation of credit scores.

Annual fee – A fee charged by a credit card company just for using their card.

Annual Credit Report Request Service – A government-backed organization that provides free annual copies of credit files.

Annual Percentage Rate (APR) – The amount of interest you will be charged on a credit card over a one year period.

Authorized use – Giving another user access to a line of credit.

Available credit – The amount of money you are allowed to spend, minus what you've already spent.

Balance transfer – When another credit card company pays off existing debt by moving the balance to a new card.

Bankruptcy – If you are unable to pay back money owed despite your best efforts, you can file for bankruptcy protection.

Bankruptcy Abuse Prevention and Consumer Protection Act (BAP-CPA) – A set of laws that places restrictions on bankruptcy filings and helps prevent consumers from abusing the right to declare bankruptcy.

Card services provider – Companies like Visa and Mastercard, who issue credit cards but do not provide the credit.

Cash advance – An amount your credit card issuer will allow you to take as cash from your available credit.

Catalog card – A credit card that is issued along with a catalog. The card may only be used to order items found within the pages of the catalog.

Charge card – Just like a credit card, except the balance must be paid in full at the end of each month.

Check-cashing business – Businesses that offer consumers without bank accounts a way to cash in their paychecks. They also offer risky payday loans, and they are not subject to government regulations.

Cosigner – a third party to a loan who guarantees that the loan gets repaid.

Credit agreement – the contract between the consumer and the agency that issues credit.

Credit counselor – a business or person who helps you manage your debt by creating a plan for dealing with it.

Credit file – A file belonging to a consumer that contains both public and private records.

Credit Karma – A company established in 2007 that allows its subscribers to view their credit reports and scores from TransUnion and Equifax for free 24/7, and provides other monitoring and mentoring services.

Credit limit – The total amount of money a creditor will allow you to spend.

Credit report – A report based on the contents of your credit file which creditors use to determine whether or not they wish to give you credit.

Credit reporting agencies – Companies that use algorithms to determine a consumer's credit-worthiness, risk, and reward to creditors, employers, and/or landlords. The three major companies are TransUnion, Equifax, and Experian.

Credit score – A score based on an algorithm that represents your credit-worthiness, risk, and reward to creditors, employers, and/or landlords.

Credit user – Categories used by creditors to determine the creditworthiness of a consumer. There are three types: true, convenience, and combination users.

Credit.com – A company that allows its subscribers to view their credit report and score from Experian for free, and provides tips for improvement.

Creditor – a person or company to whom money is owed.

Debt management plan –an ongoing intervention devised by you and your credit counselor that can take months to complete and usually requires a monthly fee to manage.

Debt-to-income model – A comparison of your income versus your expenses.

Discharged debt – debt that has been eliminated, usually by a bankruptcy filing, and which you are no longer required to pay back.

Disposable income – Money left over after paying monthly expenses, debts, and deposits into savings.

Employment history – a comprehensive listing of the jobs you have held.

Equal Credit Opportunity Act (ECOA) – A federal act establishing that women are entitled to credit in their own names if they meet the criteria.

Expenses – money that is outgoing in the form of payments made daily, weekly, or monthly.

Fair Isaac Corporation (FICO) – A California-based company that developed the most widely-accepted credit scoring model.

Finance company loans – High interest loans made by private companies with poor lending reputations.

Financial disclosures – any information that is relevant to the state of your finances, including all sources of income, and any events that have significantly influenced the state of your affairs.

Financial goals – plans you should make that will help you build, maintain, or rebuild your credit.

Financial management course – a course taught by a credit counseling agency or other educational institution that teaches good spending and saving habits.

Financial recovery company – businesses that market themselves to consumers who are attempting to recover financially from a bankruptcy filing. They usually involve training or classes of some sort for a fee.

Fixed interest rate – The rate charged for interest does not change over the life of the loan, no matter what the market is doing.

Foreclosure – The process of repossessing a property after missed or unpaid mortgage payments.

Fraud – wrongful or criminal deception that is intended to result in financial or personal gain.

Fraud alert – Notifications of activity on your financial accounts that help to cutoff potential criminal activity. These alerts can notify you almost immediately of illegal credit card purchases or withdrawals made to non-recognized accounts. If using a company's mobile application, a fraud alert can consist of something as simple as a pop-up notification

Grace period – the timeframe from when a payment is due and when a billing cycle ends.

Gross pay – what you make from your job before taxes and other deductions are made.

Identity theft – when someone uses another person's personal information for financial gain.

Income – money received, especially on a regular basis, for work or through investments.

Installment loan – financing provided over a period of time and at a set interest rate. Commonly seen at retail locations, like furniture stores, that offer high-priced merchandise.

Insurance company – a company that provides payment in the event of an accident or catastrophe, in return for regular payments from the consumer.

Interest rate – The proportion of a loan that is charged as interest to the borrower. One of the leading ways credit card companies make a profit.

Joint credit account – any type of account that is owned by more than one person. All parties on joint accounts are responsible for their settlement.

Median income – a number determined by household, and which is the amount that divides everyone into two equal groups, half having income above that amount, and half having income below it.

Medical Information Bureau – A specialty reporting agency that collects and distributes files based on your medical insurance history.

Minimum payment – the lowest amount you can pay on an outstanding debt and not be considered delinquent. Amount varies from creditor to creditor.

Mortgage – a legal agreement in which a bank or other creditor lends money to a consumer for the purchase of a home, and retains ownership of the title to said property until the debt is paid.

National check registries – A specialty reporting agency that deals with negative behavior regarding checking accounts.

Negative filing – any information that negatively impacts your credit report.

Net earnings – what you take home after taxes are withheld.

Non-installment loan – accounts where the balance must be paid in full at the end of each month.

Non-profit – a business that is structured in such a way that all earnings are funneled back into the organization.

One-time references – A credit file report that appears once and has a short credit history.

Passive income – income received without much effort, usually through investments or rental property. Also known as a secondary source of income.

Passport loan – A loan against money you already have in a bank account. Activity on these loans is often not reported to credit reporting agencies.

Payday loan – a very high-interest loan taken against a future paycheck, and that is issued by a check-cashing business.

Payment history – A list of past account payments held in a credit file.

Penalty fee – a fee charged by a credit card company for breach of the repayment contract. Penalty charges can include late payments, exceeding your credit limit, or paying your monthly bill with a check that doesn't clear.

Phishing – A common method of identity theft involving a stranger pretending to be someone else in an effort to steal personal information.

Positive cash flow – more money goes into a household than goes out.

Prepaid credit card – Cards that are loaded with funds at the time of purchase and which do not allow you to exceed the prepaid amount.

Primary source of income – the main way in which a consumer makes their money, usually through salary, tips, overtime pay, or royalties.

Reaffirmation – Proving to a bankruptcy court that you have the means to repay money owed.

Rent-to-own account – An account, usually with a retail establishment, where you pay to borrow a product or goods, and over time you will pay off the debt and own the item.

Revolving loan – the type of loan issued by credit card companies. With this type of loan you have the option of paying the bill in full each month, or carrying a balance forward with you to the next month.

Scoring model – A complex set of algorithms and calculations that process the information from your credit report and deliver a three digit score as the result.

Secured credit card – A credit account linked to a savings account in a bank. It works just like any other credit card, but the credit limit is tied to the amount of funds available in your savings account.

Security freeze – prevents credit reporting agencies from making new inquiries into your account. It will not affect accounts that are already established in your credit file.

Set-up fee – Fee charged by a credit counseling company to cover costs associated with handling your debt management plan.

Short-term cash loan – type of loan offered by pawnshops. A small amount of cash, usually a fraction of what the goods are really worth, is offered in exchange for obtaining the money very quickly and for not requiring a credit inquiry.

Specialty credit cards – Cards offered by some companies that are usually limited to purchases on specific types of goods offered by the card issuer. For example, airlines, gas stations, hotels, and retail store cards.

Spyware – a computer program that is downloaded without your knowledge. It scans your computer for valuable pieces of account information like passwords or access codes.

Student loan – loans that can come from the federal government or from private banks or financial institutions, and which are used to cover the costs associated with higher education.

Subprime lender – an institution that specializes in lending to borrowers with a tainted or limited credit history.

Subprime loan – loans offered at a much higher interest rate to borrowers with tainted or limited credit history.

Tax lien - Unpaid tax bills attached to personal property.

Temporary lift – If you have issued a security freeze on your credit report, you can apply to have it temporarily lifted if you are considering a major purchase.

Third party accounts – Accounts that place the burden of default on you and your spouse, regardless of the name on the account.

Unsecured debt – Debt that is not attached to any physical assets. If you default on your mortgage payment or car loan, the bank can take your property so that is secured debt. If you default on your credit card payment, there is nothing for the credit card company to take away.

VantageScore – A scoring model similar to FICO but which looks at slightly different variables.

Variable interest rate – the interest rate on the outstanding balance changes to reflect the fluctuations in the marketplace.

WalletHub – A company that allows its subscribers access to their TransUnion credit report and score for free, and which provides insight into the scoring process, as well as other monitoring and mentoring services.

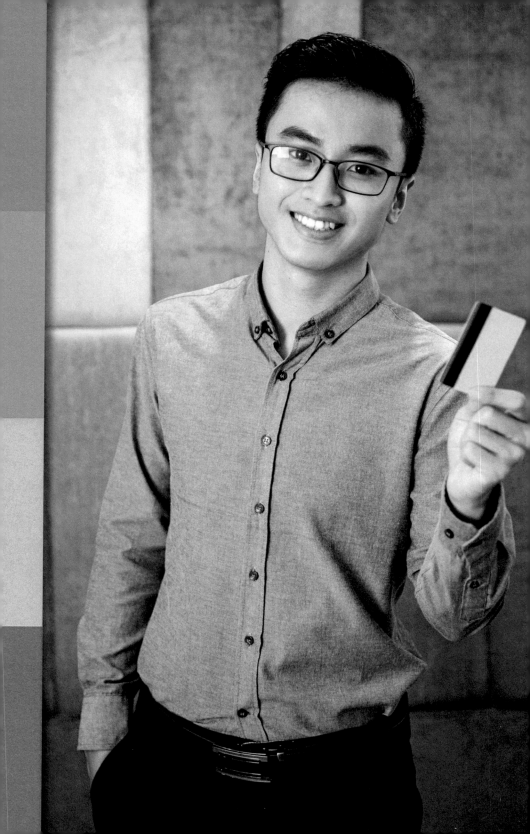

Index

Author Bio

Jeff Zschunke is a professional freelance copywriter. He has helped craft articles for charitable organizations, small businesses, and other print publications. He lives in a quiet Philadelphia suburb with his wife and two children. This is his first book.